The Pocketbook of Animal Facts & Figures

The Pocketbook of Animal Facts & Figures

Barry Kew

GREEN
PRINT

First published in 1991 by
Green Print
an imprint of The Merlin Press
10 Malden Road, London NW5 3HR

ISBN 1 85425 044 2

Typeset in Palatino 10pt by Last QT Word,
Aberdeenshire

Printed in England by Biddles Ltd., Guildford, Surrey
on recycled paper.

For those who love the source of what they hate

In Memoriam
Stan K
Ellis & Daphne K
Bob M
Mike T

CONTENTS

LIST OF TABLES

Table   **Page**

ACKNOWLEDGEMENTS

I am indebted to many people and organizations — none of them, as far as I'm aware, responsible for any errors in the text — for their assistance, generosity, information and advice, especially Simon Baker, John Bryant, Caroline Clough, Joyce D'Silva, John Elliott, Richard Farhall, Kevin Flack, Colin & Lis Howlett, Mark Glover, Mark Gold, Julie Gray, Gill Langley, Marianne Macdonald, David Martley, Marilyn & Paul Newton, Stefan Ormrod, John F. Robins, Hugh Rose, Jim Sutcliffe, Noël Sweeney.

Aberdeen Association for the Prevention of Cruelty to Animals, Aberdeen University Dept. of Agriculture Library, Advocates for Animals, ADAS, Agricultural & Food Research Council, Animal Aid, Animal Christian Concern, Animal Concern (Scotland), Animaline, Association of Agriculture, Association of Agriculture Scotland, Association of Circus Proprietors, Beauty Without Cruelty, Blackwell Scientific Publications, British Angora Goat Society, British Association for Shooting & Conservation, British Camelids Owners & Breeders Association, British Commercial Rabbit Association, British Deer Farmers Association, British Deer Society, British Deer Society (Scottish Section), British Field Sports Society, British Goat Society, British Rabbit Federation, British Trout Association, British Trust for Ornithology, British Union for the Abolition of Vivisection, British Veterinary Association, Campaign for the Abolition of Angling, Campaign Against Leather & Fur, Captive Animals' Protection Society, Care for the Wild, Cashmere Breeders Association, Chickens' Lib, CDB2 Customs & Excise, College of Estate Management (Reading University), Compassion in World Farming, Dr Hadwen Trust for Humane Research, Dept. of Agriculture (N. Ireland), Dept of the Environment, DHSS (N. Ireland), Environmental Investigation Agency, Fish Conservation Centre, Fauna & Flora Preservation Society, Food from Britain, Forestry Commission Wildlife & Conservation, Friends of the Earth, Friends of the

Earth Scotland, Game Conservancy, Goat Advisory Bureau, Goat Welfare, Goatmeat Producers Ltd, Greyhound Rescue, HM Inspectorate of Pollution, HMSO, Heretic Books, Home Office, Humane Slaughter Association, Hunt Saboteurs Association, Institute of Fisheries Management, International Fund for Animal Welfare, League Against Cruel Sports, London Food Commission, Lynx, Macaulay Land Use Research Institute, MAFF, Meat & Livestock Commission, Milk Marketing Board, National Anglers' Council, National Anti-Vivisection Society, National Dairy Council, National Farmers Union Scotland, National Federation of Zoological Gardens, National Rivers Authority, Nature Conservancy Council, Operation Fur Factory, Pet Food Manufacturers' Association, Pet Trade & Industry Association, Puppy Watch, Quaker Concern for Animals, Red Deer Commission, Rowett Research Institute, Royal Agricultural Society of England, Royal College of Veterinary Surgeons, Royal Society for the Protection of Birds, RSPCA, Scottish Agriculture College Advisory Service, Scottish Cashmere Producers Association, Scottish Milk Marketing Board, Scottish SPCA, Scottish Wildlife Trust, Sea Fish Industry Authority, SOAFD, Traffic International, Ulster SPCA, Universities Federation for Animal Welfare, Vegan Society, Vegetarian Society, Welsh Agriculture Dept, Whale & Dolphin Conservation Society, World Conservation Monitoring Centre, World Wide Fund for Nature, Zoo Check, Zoological Society of London.

And above all, to Sue.

ABBREVIATIONS

AI	*Artificial Insemination*
ADAS	*Agricultural Development and Advisory Service (MAFF)*
aka	*also known as*
b	*billion*
C	*Centigrade, Celsius*
cm	*centimetres*
DAFS	*Department of Agriculture and Fisheries Scotland* (now SOAFD)
dcw	*dressed carcase weight*
DoE	*Department of the Environment*
FCR	*food conversion rate,* e.g. 3kg feed needed to achieve 1kg weight gain shown here as 3.0.
g	*gram*
ha	*hectare* (2.47 acres)
HMSO	*Her Majesty's Stationery Office*
kg	*kilogram*
km	*kilometres*
MAFF	*Ministry of Agriculture, Fisheries and Food*
m	*million* or *metres*, depending on context.
m^2	*square metres*
m^3	*cubic metres*
mm	*millimetres*
N/A	*not applicable*
SOAFD	*Scottish Office Agriculture and Fisheries Department*
t	*tonnes*
/	*per* (when used as in 1.0g/bird/day); *and/or.*
x	*cross,* e.g. x breeding; *crossed with*, e.g. Friesian x Holstein. Or *by*, as in 1.0 x 2.5m
X	*Not available*

INTRODUCTION

This Pocketbook deals mainly with the UK and the information contained herein has been researched from government statistics, from the animal-using industries, and from those persons, groups and organizations which seek to end, reform or continue the practices by which animals are used by society and individuals. No arguments are presented or exercised but readers may wish to consult the Bibliography for sources of such and for further information on particular subject areas.

The Pocketbook cannot possibly be guaranteed to be *entirely* up to date in all its aspects as publication has to wait, in the interests of topicality, for government statistics on animal experimentation which are not released until July (and relate to the preceeding year; in this case to 1990). Other figures, compiled prior to this date, may be *slightly* dated but not by so much as to make them anything less than part of the most comprehensive single-volume guide to the use of animals in the UK.

The Pocketbook is not intended as an encyclopaedia or a study in depth, but rather as an introduction to the scale and way of things. For instance, the outline of rearing patterns in the livestock industry deals merely with those most common and/or as things are supposed to be, according to current legislation and recommendations; animals are to be found in better and worse conditions than those shown here. In different areas of the UK, different patterns will be found. With some animals, e.g. pigs, there are almost as many styles of rearing as there are farmers. With sheep especially, farm location and local conditions determine widely varying practices. None of the farmed animal chapters are intended as a practical guide to rearing livestock and nor are the surgical operations and animal disease listings offered here as a short-cut to veterinary science.

The Pocketbook is not aimed at the specialist. It is a ready, quick reference for the layperson, and readers are encouraged to progress to a study of more expert works on individual topics, not only from a factual point of view but in relation to the ethics of using animals for human purposes.

It is hoped that the Pocketbook will be regularly updated, and possibly expanded to include facts and figures on, for instance, animals used in racing, and with a greater use of tables and charts, many of which which have had to be withheld from this edition.

I would be grateful for readers' reactions. What do you think of the Pocketbook? What else might be included, and what excluded? How might the organization of material be improved for easier consultation? More importantly, any inaccuracies and errors should be pointed out for correction in future editions.

Specific references are given only where the facts, figures and/or descriptions are from a single source. Except for statistics shown under cattle, pigs, poultry, sheep, fisheries, fish farms and wild deer — which are collected by government census or regular count — the farmed animal populations shown in text and tables are estimates from the organizing, governing or opposing bodies. All 1990 MAFF figures must be regarded as provisional and invariably exclude estimates for minor holdings entirely or for those in Scotland and N. Ireland.

Finally, readers may find the text somewhat *staccato* as the emphasis on facts and figures rather than style.

1.1

COUNTRY SPORTS: ANIMALS

About 5m people take part in country sports in the UK; including some 3.7m anglers, nearly 0.5m people actively supporting hunting throughout the year, and about 0.75-1m shooters. There are approx. 54,000 shoots and hunts and fishing clubs. Country sports are also known as field sports or blood sports.

Background details of some of the animal species involved are outlined below.

BADGER (*Meles meles*)

Numbers: approx. 250,000.

0.75-0.9m long plus 0.12m tail. 0.3m at shoulder. Greyish fur, black underparts and legs. White head with black band from each ear, through eye stopping approx. 30mm from muzzle. Home known as set (sett). Eats earthworms, plants, insects, small mammals.

Mating throughout most of year, especially Feb-March, but delayed implantation process means (2-3) cubs born January-April. Cubs stay with parents. Can live over 12 years.

BIRDS[1]

Blackgame. Black Grouse (*Tetrao tetrix*)

Numbers: 10-50,000 breeding pairs in wild. (Up to 100,000 wintering birds). Mainly Scotland.

Male 0.53m long; female 0.35m. Male has lyre-shaped tail, white underneath. Female grey-brown. Sedentary.

Nests on ground. Lays late April-June. One brood. 6-11 eggs. Incubation 27 days. Chicks fly at 2-3 weeks, still growing.

Eats heather, bilberry, birch buds, conifer shoots, insects.

Capercaillie (*Tetrao urogallus*)

Numbers: 1-2,000 birds in wild. Scotland only. Extinct mid-18th century. Re-introduced (from Sweden) in 19th century.

Male 0.84m; female 0.63m. Up to about 7kg. Fan tail (turkey-like). Grey-black plumage, dark green breast, brown-tinged wings. Female ruddy brown, mottled.

Nests on ground. Lays mid April-early July. One brood. 7-11 eggs. Incubation 28 days. Chicks flutter at 2-3 weeks.

Eats pine needles, conifer shoots, fruits and bilberries, insects. Sedentary.

Partridge (Grey) (*Perdix perdix*)

Numbers: 500,000 breeding pairs in wild. Below 1m wintering birds. Originally imported from central Europe; also native.

Brown plumage, chestnut flanks and tail; neck and underparts grey; dark horseshoe on chest. Male more boldly marked. 0.3m in length.

Nests on ground. Lays late April-early June; 12-18 eggs, with repeat clutches into August. Incubation 24 days. Chicks fly at 10-11 days.

Eats grain, buds, leaves, chickweed, seeds, insects. Winters in coveys. Sedentary.

Also **Red-legged Partridge** (*Alectoris rufa*). Slightly smaller than the grey. Reintroduced from France about 200 years ago. Black and white eye stripes. No horseshoe mark on breast. Strongly barred flanks.

Pheasant (*Phasianus colchicus*)

Numbers: 100-500,000 breeding pairs in wild. (8-12m wintering birds). Originated in SW Asia. Probably introduced into Europe from Asia by Romans. Most widely distributed game bird in UK.

Male 0.84m long (incl. tail 0.45m); female 0.58m (incl. tail 0.22m). Cock mainly copper plumage, often green, grey and black-barred; hen browner. Nests on ground. Woodlands, shrubland. Lays late April-June. 8-15 eggs. Incubation 22-27 days. Chicks fly at 12-14 days. Eats fruits, seeds, leaves, leatherjackets, caterpillars, worms etc; occasionally small rodents, birds.

Ptarmigan (*Lagopus mutus*)

Numbers: approx 10,000 breeding pairs in wild. 10-15,000 wintering birds. Scotland only. Seldom below 2,000 ft.

0.35m long. Summer: white wings, dark body. Winter: pure white except for black tail. Male marked black across eye. Nests on ground near rock. Grassland, cereal lands. Lays May-June. 5-9 eggs. Incubation 21-24 days. Chicks fly at 10 days.

Eats mountain plant shoots, fruit, leaves; insects.

Red Grouse (*Lagopus lagopus*)

Numbers: approx. 500,000 breeding pairs in wild. 1.5m wintering birds.Sub-species *Lagopus scoticus* native of and possibly unique to UK. Male 0.38mlong; female 0.34m. Dark wings and tail. Male's body dark red-brown; female's browner and more barred.

Nests on ground. Lays March-June. One brood, but re-lays if first clutch lost early in incubation. 6-9 eggs. Incubation 23 days. Chicks fly at about 13 days. Eats ling shoots and seedheads, bell heather blooms, fruits and shoots of crowberry and bilberry, corn, insects. Sedentary.

DEER

Antlers worn by males only. 6 species of deer live wild in UK. No natural predators (except perhaps eagles preying on calves in Scotland) since the extinction of wolf, lynx and bear.

Chinese Water Deer (*Hydropotes inermis*)

Escaped into wild from deer parks and private collections. 0.50m at shoulder. No antlers. Males have long canine teeth. Summer coat: light reddish-brown. Winter: sandy to dark brown. Rut in Nov-Dec. Gestation 176 days. Up to 5 young, born May-July. Female has 4 teats (mammae) instead of usual 2 for deer. Eats sedges, grasses and bramble.

Fallow Deer (*Dama dama*)

Numbers: below 10,000. Introduced by Romans or Normans. Densest populations now in SE England.

Adult male (buck) approx. 0.9m at shoulder, female (doe) slightly less. Summer coat, reddish-fawn with white spots. Winter coat darker, no spots.

Palm-shaped antlers. No sign of antlers in first year. In second year fawn grows short prongs and is known as a pricket. Antlers increase in size each year, up to approx. 0.75m long. Shed in April-June. Eats grass, foliage, herbage, green twigs.

Rut in autumn. Gestation 229-240 days. Fawns (usually 1 but may be 2 or 3) born in May-June. Can live up to 15 years. Ave. 10.

Muntjac Deer (Rib-faced deer, Barking deer)(*Muntiacus reevesi*) Escaped into wild from Woburn and Whipsnade. Most now in S. England & S. Wales.

About 0.5m at shoulder. Red-brown in summer, darker in winter. Chin, throat and underside of tail white. Tusk-like canine teeth. Two short-tined antlers on long pedicles. Gestation 210 days. Fawn born any month. Eats grass, fruits, roots and browses brambles, twigs.

Red Deer (*Cervus elaphus*)

Numbers: 400,000; approx. 300,000 in Scotland (at about 10-25/km^2). Britain's largest mammal, living mainly on Scottish Highlands; an unnatural environment for a species favouring woodland. Introduced in 19th century for sporting purposes.

Adult male (stag) approx. 1.2m at shoulder, female (hind) slightly less. Summer coat reddish-brown. Winter coat brownish-grey.

Tined antlers. Male calf at few months grows pair of knobs (bossets) on head and is known as knobber. Second year these grow longer and pointed, young deer then called a brocket. In succeeding years deer known as spayad, bay, hart, stag (sixth year). Antlers up to approx. 1.1m long, weighing up to approx. 9kg. Shed in March-April. Eats soft greens, leaves, heather, grasses, sedges, herbs.

Antlers growing (in velvet) in spring-summer. In autumn, velvet is shed, antlers are hard, deer restless and stag bells. Harems formed in autumn (October) rut. Gestation about 233 days. Calves born singly — males and females in even numbers — May-June. Hind calves first at about 2 years of age. 40-45 calves/100 hinds; mortality about 25%. Natural mortality for herd up to 60% (mostly Feb-March; the very old and young).

Can live up to 17-20 years.

Roe Deer (*Capreolus capreolus*)

Numbers: Approx. 150-200,000. Overhunting exterminated roe in England & Wales by 18th century. Survived in Scotland and now occupy much of England again. Smallest native deer. Social, polygamous units of buck, doe and doe's young of the season.

Approx. 0.7m at shoulder (adult buck). 3-tined antlers up to 0.3m long, dropped Oct-Dec, renewed by February.

Summer coat: short; fox red. Winter: longer, thicker; speckled grey-fawn. White tail-patch. Young roe heavily spotted. Eats grass, leaves, shoots, buds, twigs.

Rutting season July-Aug. Gestation almost 10 months; delayed implantation. 1-2 young born May-June. Mortality about 50%.

Sika Deer (Japanese deer)(*Cervus nippon*)

Numbers: 6-10,000, mainly in Scotland. Introduced at Regent's Park in 1860 and later to others. Many escapes.

Approx. 1.05m at shoulder. 4-tined antlers up to 0.75m long. Summer: yellowy-red with white spots. Winter: black-brown. Eats grasses, heather. Rut Sept-Oct. Gestation 217 days.Young born spring.

FOX. Red Fox (*Vulpes vulpes*)

Numbers: approx. 200,000 at each January; up to 500,000 each spring (when cubs born).

Approx. 0.6m long plus brush (tail) approx. 0.45m. Tail tip (tag) often white. Height approx. 0.3m.

Coat sandy-red-brown, underparts white-ish, legs and backs of ears brown-black. Pointed muzzle. Large, erect ears. Large eyes, vertical pupil.

Approx. 1 dog + 3 vixens/400ha. Mainly nocturnal but out in day especially in fine weather. Home known as earth, but will share badger set. Eats rodents, carrion, insects, grass, fruit, veg.

Mating Dec-Feb. Gestation 51-60 days. Average litter 4 in March-April. Dog-fox feeds vixen after birth of litter. Cubs leave earth at approx. 4 weeks. Vixen takes cubs foraging. Stable family groups. Some cubs (usually males) may leave parents Aug-Nov for itinerant life before finding new territory.

Can live up to approx. 12 years but most die much earlier.

HARE. Brown Hare (*Lepus europaeus*)

Female (doe) approx. 0.55m long plus tail 100mm. Male (jack-hare) slightly smaller. Coat tawny, reddish shoulders and flanks (jack redder at shoulder). Yellowish at side of face and outer leg. Underparts white except breast and loins. Tail black above, white below and sides. Black-tipped ears. Long hind legs.

Usually solitary except breeding season. Nocturnal. No burrow. Lies in hollow (form) in grass etc. Eats grass, crops etc.

Gestation 40-44 days. About 3 litters of 1-4, Feb-Oct. Make own forms early. Mother visits to suckle. Independent at 1 month. Can live up to 12 years.

MINK (American Mink) (*Mustela vison*)

(See also **FUR FARMING** chapter).

Introduced here from N. America in 1929 by fur trade. Market collapsed in 1940/50s; mink released into wild. MAFF eradication campaign ineffective.

Male approx. 0.4-1.8kg. 0.3-0.5m long plus tail up to 0.2m. Female about two-thirds size. Coat dark brown, white chin-throat. (Has been bred with platinum, pearl and topaz coats).

Mainly nocturnal or crepuscular; solitary. Keen swimmer in wooded marsh areas. Covers approx. 9ha marshland territory or 1-4km linear riverbank. Eats small mammals, birds, frogs, crayfish, fish, snakes etc.

Mating Feb-March. Gestation 40-76 days. Litters of 3-10. Weaned at 24-35 days. Leave parents at 6-10 weeks. Can live up to 11 years.

COUNTRY SPORTS: ANGLING

(See also **FISHERIES** chapters).

The catching or taking of fish on a rod and line (an angle) and hook with bait. Hook impaled in the mouth. Fish hooked elsewhere in body known as 'foul-hooked'. Approx. 3.5-4m people go angling; 25% take part in game fishing. There are several forms of angling.

Coarse Angling (16 June-14 March with local variations)
Quarry are freshwater fish; barbel, common bream, common carp, crucian carp, chub, dace, perch, roach, tench, eels, gudgeon, bleak, ruffle, lamprey, pike. Fish largely inedible and usually returned to water. Pike and eels (often caught accidentally) generally not returned to water but killed. Eels tend to swallow bait and hook too deep for recovery. Killed by bludgeoning and severing backbone with knife.

Natural bait used including larvae (live maggots) of several flies, e.g. bluebottle, which are artificially bred and reared. Dead maggots also used; killed by plunging into hot water. Other baits: bread, worms, cheese, wheat, hemp, wasp grubs, slugs, soft fruit, tinned meat, long-dead, freshly killed and live fish, and worms — also impaled on hooks. Samples of bait thrown into water with bread, cereals to create attractive cloud (ground baiting, pre-baiting). Other baits: wooden, plastic or metal spinners or plugs armed with one or more hooks. River bottom raked over to disturb midge larvae etc. to attract fish, e.g. tench.

Hooks: singles, doubles, trebles. Conventionally barbed — some barbless — and range from about 2mm to 1cm and upwards between point and shank, removed from mouth of caught fish by hand, forceps or disgorger. Some fish swallow the hook. A 'gag'is used to keep pike's mouth open whilst retrieving hook(s).

Anglers aim to catch large fish or large numbers of fish. To avoid line breakage, fish usually have to be 'played'; fish exhausted by swimming against controlled tension through rod, line and reel. Often finally brought to bank in landing net; pike sometimes by use of gaff. In angling competition, caught fish are held captive, after hook removal, in keep-nets until match is over (3-5 hours), weighed, possibly photographed, and still-live ones returned to water when the played-out fish are at risk of attack by predators. The period in keep-net can lead to suffocation, spread of disease and victimization of smaller fish.

Coarse fish stocking carried out by moving naturally produced specimens from place to place.

Game Fishing (see Tables for seasons)

Salmonids (salmon, rainbow trout, brown trout, sea trout and grayling; fish equipped with adipose fin). Taken for the table — except undersized, non-migratory trout and salmon parr.

Fly fishing technique used, usually in fast-flowing, clean waters but also in river pools and lakes. 'Fly' made from feather, silk, wool, fur, tinsel etc. dressed on single, double or treble hooks. Other, natural, baits also used to lesser extent.

Salmon and sea trout are taken when returning to native rivers to spawn. Trout (as large coarse fish) landed in net. Salmon landed by use of gaff — stout hook, mounted on a staff, impaled through jaw or body — or by 'tailer' — staff and tapering cable-wire/running noose looped over tail of played-out fish, and pulled tight. Trout and salmon killed by blow to head with stick, stone or club ('priest'). Other fish are killed by being thrown onto hard ground, by spinal section, or by breaking spinal column.

Game fisheries are re-stocked by hatchery-reared fish, especially trout for artificial still waters. Predatory fish and birds are killed to protect game species.

Scottish angling catch of wild salmon and grilse (fish which have spent only one winter at sea) approx. 71-100,000/year. Scottish trout: approx 50,000/year.

Sea Angling (no close season)

Salt water species — bass, tope, conger, mackerel, skate, cod, pollack, ling, turbot, sole, plaice, dogfish, shark etc. — caught from shore, pier, rocks, sea walls, boats (up to about 20 miles out). Bait natural — live or dead — mainly lug, ragworm, peeler crab, molluscs, flesh from herring, mackerel, sand eels, squid; pulped fish offal. Also artificial baits dressed on hook(s).

Hooks larger and tackle sturdier than used in coarse angling. Large fish landed or brought into boat by use of gaffs and, for sharks, ropes.

Much competition fishing. Fish rarely returned to sea but delivered up dead or dying through severe injury, asphyxiation —sharks known to vomit up entire intestines in effort to get rid of hook — or killed by blows to behind vent, to skull or to snout. Sharks killed by heavy blows with lead-weighted priest or hammer to snout, just in front of eyes.

Problems and Effects

Removal from water, handling and transporting fish can damage their waterproof mucus covering (epidermis, integument). Severe damage to epidermis can result in osmotic breakdown, circulatory failure or extensive skin infection and death. Subjection to air pressure can lead to bleeding from gills.

Miles of discarded fishing line (usually a non-biodegradable nylon monofilament) and millions of lost lead weights and hooks become a threat to fish, birds, e.g. swan poisoning, and other wildlife. Some sizes of lead weights used for coarse fishing are now illegal.

Wading birds like oystercatchers, knot, dunlin, redshank, curlew are increasingly denied access to low tide food as commercial bait diggers lift between 1-3,000 lugworms/day from around the UK coast to sell to tackle shops.

COUNTRY SPORTS: COURSING

Run by the National Coursing Club and followed by approx.
1,000 people. About 500 owners run 1,000 dogs in over 22 clubs.
Approx. 2,200 courses are run/year.

Coursing dates from 1776 in Britain. Many horserace courses
had their origins in hare coursing — Kempton Park, Haydock,
Newcastle, Plumpton, Wye were founded for park coursing.

Pursuit of quarry by sight, by gazehounds — greyhounds,
whippets, deerhounds, wolfhounds, borzois, Afghans, salakis.

Premier trophy is the Waterloo Cup (end of February-early
March), held at Altcar, near Ormskirk. About 60 dogs involved.
Prize money.

Two dogs — usually greyhounds — compete against each other
in pursuit of hare.

Hare driven by crowd of beaters into coursing field. Two dogs
released by the 'slipper', giving the already-tired hare up to about
70m start. A mounted judge awards points to each dog, based on
ability to turn hare.

Hare may or may not escape (into long grass or down hole).
Both dogs often catch hare. Tug of war ensues, can last 30 seconds
or so. Interrupted sometimes by 'pickers up' reaching dogs,
taking hare and breaking its neck.

Approx. 600-1,000 hares killed in coursing annually (Sept-
March).

1.4

COUNTRY SPORTS: FALCONRY

The Wildlife & Countryside Act 1981 made it law to ring and register every bird of prey in captivity, and for keepers of such birds to be registered. Owls are not included in the registering provision. Captive barn-owl population approx. 20-30,000 (more than double the wild population).[1]

Department of Environment must be notified of every egg laid. 10-13,000 diurnal birds of prey (raptors) are kept by approx. 10,000 people in Britain. A minority, probably around 4-500, reckoned to be falconers — people who fly raptors to take live game.

The practice involves training a bird of prey to return to falconer after killing other birds, e.g. blackbirds, pigeons, larks, pheasant, grouse, or rabbits and hares. Raptors are also used as 'pest' controllers — killing certain birds or frightening birds away from specified area.

Early training can involve bird catching a lure (e.g. chick corpse) whirled on a line or dragged along ground: or 'entering' — attacking live bait (e.g. chicken) staked out on leash.

Birds used: kestrel, gyrfalcon, merlin, owl, peregrine, buzzard, lanner, sparrowhawk, saker, Harris hawk (which will hunt in teams) etc. Bells are ringed to leg or tail, or birds fitted with transmitters so can be radio-tracked to locate when straying.

When not in use, kept tethered on perches in houses, gardens, cages, aviaries; often hooded.

Illegal traffic in birds of prey for falconry.

1.5

COUNTRY SPORTS: FERRETING

Hunting rabbits with ferrets. All year round.

One or more loose-running female ferrets (jills) are released into rabbit burrow or warren to flush rabbit out to be shot, or trapped in nets set up over all escape holes. If rabbit does not bolt, and jill and rabbit remain underground, male ferret (hob) is sent down hole on a line (or with electronic tag) to locate jill (who may or may not return above ground) and kill rabbit. Ferreter then digs down to where hob (who will usually remain with the kill) is estimated to be. Some jills are never located.

Rabbits are sometimes moved from difficult working situations to easier ones by stinking out with tar- or creosote-soaked newspapers stuffed into most, not all, holes.

Ferrets bought-in (sent in boxes all over the country by rail, road) and/or home-bred. When not at work, ferrets (sometimes muzzled) kept in hutches, sheds; males and females separate.

1.6

COUNTRY SPORTS: HUNTING

The pursuit of quarry with specially-bred hounds. Most mounted hunts have foot followers. There are no legal rights to hunting; hunts are only allowed where permission is given by landowner or where hunt possesses 'sporting rights'.

The Co-op and approx. 120 local authorities have banned hunting on their land. On 8 July 1990, the Church of England's General Synod amended a private member's motion, sponsored by the Archdeacon of Colchester, the Ven. Ernest Stroud, calling for an end to hunting for sport and factory farming on the Church's 70,000ha of farm land and forest. The amendment asks the Church's Board of Social Responsibility for 'a statement of Christian stewardship in relation to the whole of creation'. A Working Party was formed by the Board.

There are no statistics to indicate how many hunts ride across Church land but most of the 194 packs registered with the Master of Foxhounds Association would have been affected.[1]

In 1990, National Trust members voted to ban stag hunting on Trust land (68,679 votes to 63,985) but rejected a ban on fox, hare and mink hunting (69,324 votes to 63,191). On 13 December 1990, the Trust's ruling council decided to let deer hunting continue on Trust land for at least another 3 years while a working party considers the implications of such a ban. Another inquiry will take place into fox hunting.[2] The NT (which has a membership of 2m) owns 6,700ha of land over which deer are hunted.

Badger
Protected species. Badger set is not protected yet (see **Appendix G: LAWS**). Terriers sent down set to attack badger. Diggers then dig through roof of set to expose fight. Fight ends when badger is clubbed with spade. Or badger forced into long fight against a pack of terriers. Approx 9-10,000 badgers/year killed thus.[3]

Badger baiting (illegal since 1835). Captured badger is chained to stake or confined in pit. Dogs encouraged to attack badger. Badger exhausted, mutilated by fight; clubbed to death. Dogs also suffer injury. Badger's jaw broken or teeth smashed before baited.

Badger drawing (illegal). Badger put in barrel, pipe or box and a succession of dogs sent in to lock in combat. 'Winner' is fastest dog to 'draw' badger out. Badger often kept for further drawing.

Deer

Deer's only natural predators, the wolf, lynx, bear, were hunted to extinction by humans. Deer are hunted from horseback with dogs. It's illegal to hunt deer with dogs in Scotland.

Tiverton Staghounds, Quantock Staghounds and Devon & Somerset Staghounds hunt the red deer (killing approx. 150/ year; around 1 kill every 2 outings); New Forest Buckhounds hunt the fallow deer males (bucks), (killing 5-10/year).

A suitable (warrantable) deer is located by the hunt's 'harbourer'. Tufters scent out the chosen (harboured) stag and start the chase. (Deer may have to be separated from herd first). Stag begins to emit scent stronger than other deer. Scent followed by other hounds (pack is 'laid on') after about 1 hour. In early stages, the stag outpaces the hounds but tires and seeks refuge, often in cover (but will go through streams, into farms and gardens). Chased out by huntsmen, whippers-in, riders, foot followers.

After several hours, the stag's stamina is drained. Hounds are more enduring. Usually, after up to about 40km (maybe 7 hours), stag seeks final sanctuary in stream, river, slope, thicket (standing at bay). Hounds close in. Stag defends himself with antlers. Riders catch up. Stag shot. Alternatively, stag brought to bay in open field and shot.

Same routine with hind, but cannot defend herself with antlers. Dogs may close in before riders arrive. Hinds may be pregnant and with previous year's calf at foot. Calf tires early and is often taken by hounds.

After the kill, deer's stomach is slit open. Offals are cut up and distributed amongst hunt followers. Heart goes to owner of land where deer killed. Legs skinned and broken off. Feet given or sold to supporters. Teeth removed, sold as mementoes. Antlers given to hunt friends. Meat distributed. Hounds called in to eat entrails.

The practice of 'carted deer' hunting continues in N. Ireland. A captive, de-antlered and possibly castrated stag is taken to countryside in 'cart' and released for hounds and following riders to chase to exhaustion. Then caught and carted back to paddock. May be thus hunted several times/season.

Fox

There are approx. 194 fox-hunts in UK (Scotland's oldest hunt — the Linlithgow and Stirlingshire — closed down in 1991 after 225 years), each hunting 2-4 days/week over large areas (e.g. Cottesmore Hunt: 3,110km^2; Heythrop: 1,814km^2). Most of UK is covered; each hunt having on average about 1,000 separate farms in its area. Foxes are usually hunted from horseback. Hunts kill approx. 12-16,000 foxes/year and are partially funded by receipts from point-to-point races. Other foxes are killed by (approx. annual figs): snare (100,000); gun (100,000); road accidents, natural causes, local authorities (60,000); terrier men (30,000).

An average fox-hunt might keep about 60 hounds, bred for stamina, not speed; 10-30 used in each hunt. 30-200 people in main body of riders, led by Master. Accompanied by followers on foot and/or in vehicle. Terrier men also, for when fox 'goes to ground'.

Foxes are nocturnal, so are still often out of their earth very early in morning when 'earth stoppers' go out to block fox earth entrances. Foxes thus forced to stay 'above ground'. Most hunts gather late morning and move off to promising location, hounds ahead to flush out fox. Chase begins. Fox outpaces hounds at first. Will go through woods, across tracks, gardens etc. Hounds in full cry will attack and kill pets and other animals. Fox's stamina wanes. Caught and savaged ('broken up') by hounds or goes to ground in unblocked earth or badger set. Not safe underground. Terrier men called in.

Terrier men put terrier dogs down earth or set to 'bolt' fox. Fox either emerges and chase commences, or fox stays put. If latter, terriers keep up attack and terrier men dig fox out. When exposed, fox is shot, forced to run or thrown to hounds. Hunts end around 3-4pm. Terrier men might continue digging for a fox long after riders have gone home. Also, terrier gangs are active all year round, unattached to hunts.

The season's period means that many foxes are heavily pregnant or nursing when hunted. One in 3 to one in 10 hunts end in the death of a fox. Hunts might provide artificial earths for fox breeding; leave sufficient foxes to breed next hunt quarry; transfer cubs from area to area to ensure huntable numbers. Cub-hunting takes place in August, prior to season (Nov-April).

• *Cub-hunting.* Purpose: to 'blood' young, inexperienced hounds. Quarry are fox-cubs born in spring, now approx. 5-6 months old. Hunt surrounds cub(s) in, e.g. wood, chase with hounds and horses; cub is caught and killed by hounds. Adults often allowed to escape. Cubs might also be dug out from earths for hounds.

Hare (Beagling)

Hares are hunted in UK by packs of 3 different breeds of hound: approx. 90 packs of beagles; 8 packs of bassets; 24-50 packs of harriers. 10-35 hounds/hunting pack.

Beagles and bassets are followed on foot by huntsmen, whippers-in and 'the field', over all kinds of terrain. (Harriers are followed on horseback). Each pack hunts about twice/week. Dogs are about 18 months old at first hunt.

Season Sept/Oct to March/April. Hounds are set to pick up scent and pursue hare which has no specific refuge but will leap hedges, run along top of wall etc. One out of four hares hunted is caught and killed by hounds (beaten by superior stamina, not speed). Others escape. Pack takes approx. 60-90 minutes to exhaust and kill a hare.

Approx. 2-7,000 hares/year are killed by hunts.

Mink

Hunted on foot with dogs — beagles, bassets, harriers, fell hounds, foxhounds. Mink-hunting replaced otter hunting (banned in 1978) which, along with organo-chlorine (pesticide) poisoning, brought the otter to brink of extinction.

Each hunt has one Master or two or more Joint Masters (managers). Hunt staff includes (horn-carrying) huntsman — tactics etc; whippers-in — pack control; and terriermen — use of terriers and digging when mink goes to ground. Plus hunt followers —

the field. Hunts usually meet on Saturdays, also mid-week, at 11 a.m. Evening hunts at about 5 or 6 p.m. April to Sept/October.

Hounds (about 12-18 months old at first hunt) meander up and down river banks followed on foot by hunters. Mink scented and hounds then hunt the drag (follow scent) until mink is found (in hole, lying rough, up tree). Mink is dug out or bolted or tree is cut down; mink now properly hunted. May be dug out again or caught and killed by dogs, or drowned, or shot by hunters, or lost by hounds. Hunt outing may cover about 8km. Otter at risk from dogs hunting mink and from habitat disturbance.

Approx. 15 hunts kill about 2-800 mink/year.

Concern has been expressed over the possible treatment (e.g. starving before hunt), training and disposal of all dogs used for hunting.

COUNTRY SPORTS: SHOOTING

There are 5 shooting categories involving animals as targets.

Shotguns — which kill by injury and shock of impact — are used in 4: Game Shooting; Rough Shooting; Wildfowling; Pigeon Shooting. Rifles — better targeting of specific vital area(s) — are used in the other: Deer Stalking. (Foxes are also shot. Hounds drive foxes towards line of shotguns; mainly in Wales, Highlands, and upland areas).

Dogs — English springer spaniel, golden retriever, labrador — are used to find, flush and/or retrieve injured game for a second shot or other method of despatch (e.g. blow to back of bird's head or neck dislocation).

Approx. 600,000 licence holders use shotguns regularly for shooting live quarry. Around 4,000 regularly stalk with rifle. About 120m shotgun cartridges are discharged/year in UK (3,000t of toxic lead).

Game Shooting

5 species of game bird are defined by the Game Act 1831 — blackgame, grouse, partridge, pheasant, ptarmigan. Capercaillie are also shot in this category though not defined in Act (extinct when passed). Hares defined as ground game (no game licence needed). In addition, game licence required for snipe and woodcock.

Two main styles of game shooting. Driven shooting — birds frightened, flushed from cover and driven over standing guns by teams of beaters. Walking-up shooting — guns walk in line through cover with gun dogs to help flush game. Heavy emphasis on game management.

In a flying bird the vital centre, i.e. the area to be hit by pellets, accounts for approx. 11% of the visible profile in side view. Shooters aim for heads of flying birds. Many birds are injured rather than killed as intended.

Hare

Shot in rough shoot or during 'drives': long lines of shooters beat across field or in decreasing circle, shooting any hares that get up. Generally during early spring. Upwards of 300,000 are shot/year.

Game Birds

Pheasant and partridge not native. Introduced in 11th and 17th centuries respectively.

Young pheasant and partridge are reared from adults or their eggs, taken from wild; from bought in day-olds, or from 6 week old poults. Open field, movable pens, broody hens, brooder houses or intensive rearing systems are used. Chicks or poults are gradually acclimatized to outdoor conditions and transferred to release pen at about 6-8 weeks of age.

Surgical. Measures include debeaking (re feather-pecking and cannibalism); wing-tagging, wing-clipping (retained birds); pinioning (removal of wing manus); brailing (taping one wing down); fitting spectacle 'bits' by pushing stake through nasal cavities.

Average young pheasant will eat approx. 1.25kg of crumbs and pellets up to 6 weeks of age, then 2kg pellets and wheat/month. Laying birds and cocks 3kg /month. Partridges eat 25% less.

Game bird diseases: coccidiosis, roundworms, gapeworms, hairworm, gizzard worm, tapeworm, blackhead. Problems: feather and tail pecking, toe picking, cannibalism, hysteria, panic.

Gamekeepers destroy — by trapping (incl. cage-trapping with caged call-birds; and pole-trapping), snaring, shooting, poisoning — animals and birds which constitute a threat to the game. Victims include fox, stoat, weasel, hedgehog, squirrel, mink, polecat, otter, wildcat, pinemarten, birds of prey, jay, magpie, crow, jackdaw, raven, with other, incidental deaths of cats and dogs. Rabbit or bird carcase bait is laced with poison such as Alphachloralose (rodenticide), Phosdrin and Yaltox (insecticides) and strychnine. Or eggs of bird of prey are injected with liquid poison.[1] Warfarin also used on, e.g. squirrels.

Between 1980 and 1989, 327 birds of prey and hundreds of dogs, cats, foxes and other wild animals were killed illegally with poisoned bait.[2] Between 1979 and 1989 illegal persecution by poison, trap or gun caused the deaths of at least 40 golden eagles, 65 peregrine falcons, 68 kestrels, 57 hen harriers, 39 goshawks, 24 red kites, 71 owls and 367 buzzards. Other victims included white-tailed eagles, merlins, marsh harriers and sparrowhawks.[3] Between 1971 and 1989 at least 400 buzzards, 110 peregrines, 95 sparrowhawks, 70 golden eagles, 70 hen harriers, 30 goshawks, 30 red kites and 6 ospreys were illegally trapped, shot or poisoned.[4] Over 40 rare birds were found poisoned in Scotland in 1989; 3 prosecutions.[5] In the 1890s there were about 23,000 gamekeepers; now there are 3-5,000.

Partridge and pheasant constitute approx. 90% of all game birds shot. Shot at from about 12-24 weeks of age.

Pheasant

Usually artificially hand-reared (from 7 hens to one cock adult breeding ratio; kept in pens: about 50 eggs/hen) or from incubated eggs (and sold to estates as poults or chicks). Kept in pens — fed on chick pellets, maize, kale, millet etc. and onto wheat — then released as poults into keepered woods until mature (up to 20 weeks). Broody hen incubation rarer; hens in nestboxes for 24 days up to hatching.

From about 9.30-10.00 am on days of main covert shoots (the first often into November), gunmen line the edge of a wood, beaters enter, often with spaniels, and flush birds into flight over line of shotguns. Or walk-up shooting.

Many birds fly wounded and/or fall wounded to ground. Retrieved by dogs, bird's neck then dislocated.

Up to 12m, mainly purpose-bred, birds shot/season.

Red Grouse

Totally wild. Numbers artificially swelled not by breeding but by gamekeeper control of predators (foxes, crows, gulls, stoats, rats, weasels), and management of grouse moors.

Grouse eat mainly young shoots of ling. To ensure regular supply, heather is burned rotationally in 0.8-2.5ha patches (muirburn) so moor is mixture of heather at different stages. Short growth for food, longer for cover. Disease and parasites a consequence of unnatural high density of grouse.

Birds driven into air over a line of butts (which conceal shooters) by beaters — birds shot at about 15-25m range; or walk-up shooting. Up to 0.5m birds shot/season, at about 3-4 months old.

The number of red grouse — and the 80,000 or so people who shoot them — is more or less equally divided between the Yorkshire moors and the Scottish hills.

Blackgame and ptarmigan populations are largely unmanaged. The Scottish Office decided in September 1990 against a ban on the shooting of the world's largest grouse — capercaillie — despite fears that it could face extinction.[6]

Rough Shooting

Probably the predominant shooting interest in UK. Walking up over rough land, spinneys, copses, marshes, fields etc. Little, if any, game management. Usually 1-4 people at a time, plus dogs.

The shooting of game, wildfowl, rabbits, woodpigeon and other 'opportunist' species — rooks, crows, jackdaws, magpies, jays, pigeons — seen as pests and unprotected by Wildlife & Countryside Act. No close season; a breach of European Birds Directive 1979.

Pigeons (up to approx. 12m/year), woodcock (150,000), foxes (100,000), rabbits (approx. 4m). Many killed when they have dependent young.

The Scottish Office Agriculture and Fisheries Dept. funds 29 Fox Destruction clubs which kill approx. 10,000 foxes/year by shooting, snaring, poisoning.

Wildfowling

Shooting wild geese and duck — indigenous and migratory. Normally, shooters on foot but boats also used. On foreshore or on marshes, lakes, lochs between high and low tide.

Roosting ducks are often attracted by pond excavation and landscaping. Artificial feeding is practised and some species, e.g. mallard, are often artificially reared, and released (some 400,000/year) at about 6 weeks; shot at about 18-24 months.

Birds generally shot early morning, late evening or at night as they fly between roosting and feeding grounds. Many birds ingest and are poisoned by fallen, spent lead shotgun pellets.

Wildfowlers hide in cover on wetlands, waiting for birds to fly in for breeding, feeding. Plastic or wooden decoy ducks are often set out to entice ducks. Birds shot, many not killed but wounded, falling to inaccessible places. Approx. total of 1-1.8m wildfowl of different species shot/year. About 60% mallard. Mostly inland.

In 1989, 915 Greenland barnacle geese and 45 white-ronted geese — both protected species — were shot by organized sporting parties on the Hebridean island of Islay under crop protection licence, which requires that farmers 'shoot to scare rather than shoot to kill'.[7]

Pigeon Shooting
Shooting from hide or cover. Setting out decoys, attracting pigeon to feeding ('restaurant') field. Around 12m shot/year.

Deer
Generally, shooting red deer in the Highlands (little or no tree cover); roe, fallow, sika (and crosses) and muntjac in lowlands. Illegal to kill deer with a shotgun unless serious damage is occurring and then under restrictive conditions.

In addition to sporting interests the Red Deer Commission may authorize anyone they consider competent to go on any land in Scotland to kill deer causing serious damage to forestry and agriculture, but not to flora and fauna. (Deer [Scotland] Act 1959).

Traditional shooting of deer in middle age range. Stags: 4-9 years; hinds 2-8 years old. Herd management shoots young stags and old hinds, leaving sportsmen to take mature stags. Herds and ranges are managed to provide commercial shooting (trophies and venison). Other management practices: muirburn, fertilizing, liming, re-seeding land plus winter feeding.

Shooter(s) are usually led by a professional stalker. Deer chosen and stalked; suitable shooting position achieved, and deer shot from up to 90-135m (this style especially in red deer stalking). Alternatively, position sought first and animal selected, or deer induced (by dog, beaters or call) to pass waiting marksmen. Fixed or portable 'high seats' often used to survey areas and/or to shoot from. Roe deer are stalked and shot very early morning or late evening; long stalks and shots rare.

Heart-lung shots are considered most sure and humane by some. Others favour brain shot especially at close range (or only at point blank, and not in profile), others consider neck shot more acceptable, and especially when despatching wounded animal.

Risk of damaging — e.g. windpipe or jaw — rather than killing. Night shooting restricted.

Approx. 300,000 red deer population in Scotland; 86,000 stags, 160,500 hinds, 53,500 calves. Total in 1963 was 150,000. (Mainly in Western Highlands). Approx. 320,000 nationwide.

In 1989, 20,000 stags were shot, 7,000 more than target set by the Government's Red Deer Commission.[8] About 5% of red deer in Scotland are shot out of season. Approx. 80,000 red deer are shot in England each year. Most recent Forestry Commission deer cull figures: Red 6,347; Roe 11,173; Fallow 1,962; Sika 973; Muntjac 365. Approx. 3-500 fallow deer/year shot by Forestry Commission in the New Forest.

The Red Deer Commission has called for an extra 24,000-50,000 hinds to be culled over the next few years, following an increase in the number of breeding hinds. Simultaneously, the venison market (mainly in Germany) is falling, due to glut of venison going in from the now opened-up Eastern European countries.

Deer meat is now also being turned into sausage, haggis and burgers and used in pies, stews and goulashes.

Approx. 3,000t/year venison now comes from deer shooting.

Instead of shooting red deer hinds, owners of Highland forests catch many alive (darted) and transport them (usually south) to deer farms.

Gun Use

Shotgun Certificate holders in UK	865,105
Firearm Certificate (rifles, pistols) holders	149,363
Estimated to be regular users	600,000
Shooting 'pests' (rabbits, hares, crows, foxes etc.)	340,000
Shooting wood pigeon	290,000
Shooting wildfowl, waders and ducks	160,000
Shooting driven or walked-up game birds	130,000
Those rough shooting	270,000

Of the Firearm users:

Those who regularly shoot live quarry	46,000
Those shooting deer	3-5,000[9]

Shooting in Scotland

In the past 100 years the ratio of commercial to private shooting has barely changed from the current figure of 4:1.

The vast majority of 'guns' still come from the south of England, about 25% of commercial shooting is now let to foreigners (25% American).

Estimates of the volume of game shot in Scotland 1988-89:[10]

Duck	107,639
Geese	7,933
Grouse	303,319
Partridge	36,820
Pheasant	1,019,401
Snipe	13,470
Woodcock	18,067
Other game birds	806
Hare	94,672
Pigeon	195,339
Rabbit	407,871
Red Deer	52,372
(Stags	20,823)
(Hinds	26,976)
(Calves	4,573)
Roe, Sika and Fallow Deer	12,637

No. of participants in sporting shooting (Scotland): 50,885 (of which, from Scotland16,904; Rest of UK 22,408; Rest of World 11,573). Estimated number of properties used for sporting shooting (Scotland) 3,298.[10]

Shooting Seasons

Birds
No close seasons: collared dove, crow, great black-backed gull, herring gull, jackdaw, jay, lesser black-backed gull, magpie, pigeon (feral), rook, sparrow (house), starling, woodpigeon.
  (All birds of prey are protected at all times).

Mammals
No close seasons: coypu, fox, mink, rabbit, rat (brown), squirrel (grey), stoat, weasel.

Hare
Generally shot at any time in Britain except for prohibition in England & Wales on moorlands and unenclosed non-arable land, 1 April-10 December and in Scotland, 1 April-30 June. Hares or leverets may not be offered for sale in Britain 1 March-31 July. In N. Ireland hares may be shot only during 12 August-31 January. In England & Wales it is unlawful to kill hares on a Sunday or Christmas Day.

Protected Wild Animals
At all times: badger, common otter, red squirrel.
May not be taken or killed by certain methods: hedgehog, pine marten, polecat, wild cat.

Table 1. Shooting Seasons: Deer (England & Wales)							
	Fallow		Red		Roe		Sika	
	Buck	Doe	Stag	Hind	Buck	Doe	Stag	Hind
January								
February								
March								
April								
May								
June								
July					1 Apr to 31 Oct			
August								
September								
October								
November	1 Aug to 30 Apr	1 Nov to 28 Feb	1 Aug to 30 Apr	1 Nov to 28 Feb		1 Nov to 28 Feb	1 Aug to 30 Apr	1 Nov to 28 Feb
December								
Numbers shot/year	Approx. 1200		Approx. 80,000		Approx. 2400 but see text		Approx. 75	
No close season for muntjac or Chinese water deer								

26

Table 2. Shooting Seasons: Deer (Scotland)

	Fallow		Red		Roe		Sika	
	Buck	Doe	Stag	Hind	Buck	Doe	Stag	Hind
January	▓	▓		▓		▓		▓
February	▓	▓		▓		▓		
March	▓					▓		
April	▓				1 Apr to 20 Oct			
May					▓			
June					▓			
July			1 July to 20 Oct		▓		1 July to 20 Oct	
August	▓		▓		▓		▓	
September	▓		▓		▓		▓	
October	▓		▓		▓		▓	
November	1 Aug to 30 Apr	21 Oct to 15 Feb		21 Oct to 15 Feb		21 Oct to 31 Mar		21 Oct to 15 Feb
December	▓	▓		▓		▓		▓
Numbers shot/year	Approx. 50 but see text		About 40,000 incl. 5,000 calves		Approx. 2500		Approx. 450 but see text	

Red-sika hybrids as for red and sika deer.
No close season for muntjac or Chinese water deer

Table 3. Shooting Seasons: Wild Birds				
	Coot, Moor-hen, GPlover	Snipe	Wild Duck*	Wild Geese**	Woodcock
January					
February					
March					
April					
May					
June					
July					
August					
September					
October	1 Sept to 31 Jan	12 Aug to 31 Jan. From 1 Sept in N Ireland	Inland 1 Sept to 31 Jan. Foreshore 1 Sept to 20 Feb		1 Oct to 31 Jan. From 1 Sept in Scotland.
November					
December					
Numbers shot/year	Not known	Approx. 100-150,000/ year	Approx. 1-1.8m/year		Approx. 150,000/ year

*Common pochard, gadwall, mallard, pintail, shoveller, teal, tufted duck, widgeon. **Canada, greylag, pink-footed, white-fronted (Eng/Wales only)

Table 4. Shooting Seasons: Game Birds					
Blackgame	Capercaillie	Grouse	Partridge	Pheasant	Ptarmigan
20 Aug to 10 Dec From 1 Sept in New Forest Devon & Somerset	1 Oct to 31 Jan	12 Aug to 10 Dec to 30 Nov in N Ireland	1 Sept to 1 Feb 1 Oct to 31 Jan in N Ireland	1 Oct to 1 Feb 1 Oct to 31 Jan in N Ireland	12 Aug to 10 Dec
Not known	Not known	0.5m	Approx. 0.5m	Approx. 10-12m	Not known
Illegal to kill grouse, partridge, pheasant, ptarmigan on a Sunday or Christmas day.					

Table 5. Hunting Seasons					
	Red Deer	Fallow Deer	Fox	Hare	Mink
January	Hinds	Bucks			
February	Hinds	Bucks			
March	Spring Stags				
April	Spring Stags				April to October
May			to end of May in some areas		April to October
June					April to October
July					April to October
August			Cubs 4 Aug to 1 Nov.		April to October
September	Stags		Cubs 4 Aug to 1 Nov.		April to October
October	Stags		Cubs 4 Aug to 1 Nov.	Oct to March (approx) Coursing 15 Sept to 10 Mar	April to October
November	Hinds	Bucks Sept & 1 Nov to 10 March	Nov to April	Oct to March (approx) Coursing 15 Sept to 10 Mar	
December	Hinds	Bucks Sept & 1 Nov to 10 March	Nov to April	Oct to March (approx) Coursing 15 Sept to 10 Mar	
Numbers killed/year	Approx. 1-300	Approx. 5-10	Approx. 12-16,000	Approx. 2-7,000. 600-1,000 by coursing	Approx. 2-800

Illegal to hunt deer with dogs in Scotland
Illegal to kill hares on a Sunday or Christmas Day in England & Wales

Table 6. Angling Seasons			
Char	Coarse	Salmon	Trout
1 Mar to 30 Sept	16 June to 14 March* varies in different localities	England, Wales & Scotland: 15 Jan to 31 Oct. N Ireland: 2 Feb to 30 Oct. all maximum: vary in different localities	England & Wales 1 Mar to 31 Oct. Scotland 15 Mar to 6 Oct N Ireland 2 Feb to 30 Oct Rainbow trout no national close season.
Not known	Not known	Not known	Not known
*Season does not apply to private owners of enclosed waters (ponds, lakes) where there are no feeder streams.			

FARMED ANIMALS:
BREEDING & FEEDING

General Information

There are a number of points to consider over and above those mentioned in the text.

1. That with increasing specialization in each area of livestock agriculture, any particular farmer is less and less likely to be involved in all stages of production. The industry as a whole continues to move towards a situation where farmers and companies breed, or fatten and produce. This is not to say however that many, especially larger companies, do not still do both.

2. The general trend continues to be one of fewer but larger farms.

3. The development of intensive livestock farming has steadily given rise to greater disease and behavioural problems, the former being treated with a range of pharmaceutical products.

4. Between the years 1983-1986 (the last year for which figures are available) annual animal deaths in agricultural buildings rose from 38,512 (100 fires) to 60,445 (183 fires) — about 90% poultry.[1]

5. Farmed (and other) animals are also used in experiments (e.g. at the Institute of Animal Physiology, Babraham, Cambs) to seek increased control over breeding and performance. (See also **VIVISECTION** chapter).

BREEDING

Consult also the chapters on individual farmed animal species for different practices.

The general intention of the livestock industry is to maximize output (of flesh, product or offspring) with minimum input cost in minimum time.

'Superior' animals are identified and exploited to the full. 'Inferior' animals (infertile, low yield, male etc.) are usually killed. The animals we see (or are unable to see) on farms today are the results of years, decades or centuries of specialized breeding and genetic manipulation.

Heat Periods/Oestrus

These start when or after female reaches puberty. At oestrus — at certain times of the year (e.g. ewes) or throughout the year (e.g. cows) — eggs are released from ovaries, regulated by photoperiodic signal and secretion of melatonin hormone from the pineal gland.

Length of oestrus varies with species. During oestrus, hormones are released in the blood and the womb becomes ready for a fertilized egg. At this time, the animal is known as 'on heat' or 'in season'. Oestrus period is often manipulated by artificially controlled day length, hormone injection and/or intravagination.

Artificial Insemination (AI)

Started in 1940s, and now controlled by the Milk Marketing Board (and some private centres) for cattle, and by the Meat & Livestock Commission for pigs. AI is responsible for up to 3m UK pregnancies/year. Commonest with cattle, increasingly so with pigs and other species.

Semen is taken twice weekly from bulls kept at special centres in narrow stalls. The bull is encouraged to mount a 'teaser' animal (usually a blindfolded male) several times. Penis is then inserted into an artificial leather vagina to ejaculate. The collected semen is diluted and mixed with skimmed milk, glycerol, fruit sugar, antibiotics and stored, to be later inserted manually into cow by use of inseminating gun. Bulls are exercised round a treadmill or staked in a field. Killed at approx. 12 years of age.[2] Each year

Genus inseminators carry out over 1m dairy breed inseminations, most of which are from the extensive range of Holstein x Friesians.[3] With pigs, the boar is trained to mount a dummy sow, then is hand-stimulated to ejaculate into a jar or bottle. Sow is inseminated via a catheter. Used also for sheep. (And see **FISH FARMING** chapter for other techniques).

Embryo transfer

First practised in 1890, on rabbits. Increasingly used on cattle, goats, pigs and sheep. Removal of developing embryo from female animal's uterus and transfer of it to another female for foetus development. Natural mother then able to be mated again. Maximizes number of offspring from selected breeding females. Alternatively, when some young beef heifers are slaughtered their ovaries are removed and taken to laboratory for *in vitro* fertilization of eggs with semen from high quality beef bulls. Up to 40 eggs can be taken from one heifer. The embryo is then implanted in the womb of another (surrogate mother) dairy cow. The technique enables wholly beef-bred calves to be born to dairy cows (who do not normally produce the best beef animals).

Gene Technology

Research is currently being conducted into sex predetermination; cloning; genetic reconstitution; transgenic animals, carrying genes from other species; patenting of 'new' species. Human genes have been inserted into sheep. Bovine Somatotropin (BST) is the first hormone of the new technological generation, being tested to increase cows' milk yield. (And see **VIVISECTION: Animal Supply** and **Livestock Research**, and **CATTLE: Dairy Cattle**).

FEEDING

Consult also the chapters on individual farmed animal species.

Feed is the largest single cost in livestock production — up to 80% of pig and poultry costs, 60% for cattle, 50% for sheep — and includes more than just feed; vitamin and mineral supplements and growth promoting antibiotics are also included.

Livestock feeding varies with the condition of the animal, i.e. different rations — amounts and component concentration — are given for maintenance; growth and fattening; pregnancy and lactation. All are related to body weight and dry matter content of the feed. The most important food received by the young mammal is colostrum — from the mother's first milk. Many female breeding animals are flushed and steamed up. (See **GLOSSARY**).

A ban on the feeding of selected offal (brain, spinal cord, spleen, thymus, tonsils, intestines of bovines killed over 6 months old) to all animals, including pets, was ordered by MAFF as from 25.9.90. (This extended the ban on feeding same to cattle after high incidence of BSE — see **Appendix B**).

Digestive Systems

Pig and poultry feed is almost entirely concentrates. Calves and lambs need digestible and fairly concentrated food, milk and good-quality grass when young.

Ruminants in general are fed a combination of concentrates and roughage. Highest concentrate amounts are fed to dairy cows; lowest in sheep and suckler cow feeds.

Young animals have a more efficient food conversion rate (FCR) than older animals. But in younger animals, the inedible parts of the carcase make up a greater % of the total.

Main Feed Types

Bulky Feeds — generally high in fibre and/or water.

1. Roots. Turnips, swedes, mangolds, beets, potatoes, sugar beet pulp, manioc.

2. Green forage crops. Grass. Brassicas (kale used for autumn and winter feeding, esp. dairy cattle). Rape (high protein), sugar beet tops, stubble turnips. Silage: made by preserving and fermenting green forage crops (usually grass or grass-clover) under acid conditions, excluding oxygen. Bacteria control the fermenting process, converting carbohydrate into lactic acid; a pickling process. Silage is often improved by the use of additives like molasses, formic acid or bacteria inoculants.

3. Fodder. Hay and straw from green crops harvested when fully grown (straw; usually barley) or cut early and dried (hay). Straw is often chemically treated with, e.g. sodium or ammonia (alkali), to improve feed value.

Concentrated Feeds — low in fibre and water; high energy and / or protein. The most expensive foods.

1.   Compounds. Proprietary ready-mixed foods. The commonest farm foods, balanced for the purpose, e.g. dairy nuts, ewe and lamb mixture. Approx. 10.8m tonnes were used in UK in 1990.

2.   Straights. Concentrates bought-in singly for mixing with e.g. home grown cereals. Dairy concentrate, pig breed concentrate etc. Approx. 4.6m tonnes were used in the UK in 1990. Types and examples:

(a) Cereals. Barley (finely ground) is the chief cereal fed to livestock in UK, mostly to pigs. Maize (can enhance egg yolk colour); flaked maize; wheat , highest protein — forms up to 70% of poultry diets; rye; oats (usually for cattle and sheep); sugar beet pulp; cereal pellets; sorghum.

(b) Milling and other cereal by-products. Wheatfeed — what is left (about 28%) after white flour is produced. Used in cattle and pig feeds to aid digestion. Rice bran.

Brewer's or distiller's grains — by-products, used wet or dry for dairy cows. Yeast products.

(c) Animal proteins. White fish meal made from ground-up whole white fish, incl. bones. Herring meal. Up to 60% of all fishmeals go into poultry feeds, 20% into pig feeds, the rest to ruminants and fish. Meat and bone meal. Milk powder. Offals, manures, slurries.

(d) Vegetable proteins. Peas and beans. Lupins. Dried grass and dried lucerne used in many feed mixtures, supplying carotene. Soya bean meal. Linseed cake. Rape seed meal.

(e) Nitrogen foods. Urea, used as part of compound, or incorporated in supplement blocks or liquids for ruminents to synthesize protein.

3.   Fats & oils. Feed grade animal fats (FGAF) often mixed with vegetable oils. Oilcakes and meals, made from oil seeds after the oil has been removed by crushing or by extraction (as at (d) above).

4.   Additives. Antibiotics (often acting as growth promoters). Flavourings. Colourings.

5.   Supplements. Vitamins and minerals are especially used in

indoor, intensive systems. Provided in mix or as licks or blocks. Approx. 5% of all feeds. Amino acids.

6. Other feeds. Molasses. Citrus pulp.

BOCM Silcock is the UK's largest animal feed supplier.

Water

Approx. 70 litres of water/day/head of livestock are needed for cleaning and cooling etc. In the 1980 report, *Water for Agriculture: Future Needs*, the Advisory Council for Agriculture and Horticulture estimated annual intake of water by agriculture to be 65,000m gallons (295.75b litres), 60% from public mains and 40% from private abstraction. Livestock husbandry was the largest single consumer at 35,000m gallons (159.25b litres). See feed sections in farmed animal species chapters for consumption/animal.

What Goes In...

Each year in the UK, farm animals produce about 200m tonnes of effluent (slurry; liquid manure). Example daily figures for individuals of selected species:

Heifers and dairy cows — 20-50 litres; calves — 7-14 litres; pigs 4-20 litres; sheep — 3-6 litres; 100 turkeys — 13-20 litres; 100 broilers — 8-10 litres; 100 layers — 12-14 litres.

What Goes

Since 1945, we have lost 95% of our flower-rich meadows, 50% of our ancient woodlands, 40% of our heathlands and 50% of our fens and wet valleys. 224,000km of hedgerows have been removed to accommodate modern machines and new farming practices.[4]

Timber production from UK forests accounts for 12% of the nation's requirements for wood and wood products. In 1989, the import bill for timber stood at £7.3b.[5]

(And see **FARM ANIMALS: LAND USE** Table on page 38).

Table 7. Farm Animals: Land Use[1]

The UK measures 24,475,500ha (60.5m acres).
All figures below are for hectares.

	1989	1990[2]
Area used for agricultural purposes	18.55m (75.8% of total)	18.51m (75.6% of total)

Areas of land used for livestock; grazing or feed-growing

	1989	1990[2]
Grassland for grazing, silage, hay etc.	6.78m	6.84m
Rough grazing	5.95m	5.92m
Wheat	829,822 (of 2.08m total wheat)	836,006 (of 2.01m total wheat)
Barley	827,869 (of 1.65m total barley)	790,595 (of 1.51m total barley)
Oats	45,618 (of 118,600 total oats)	47,887 (of 106,500 total oats)
Peas	72,300	67,200
Field beans	129,000	139,200
Turnips/swede	51,000	46,300
Beets/mangolds	10,700	11,500
Kale, cabbage, kohl rabi, rape	25,200	24,400
Others	9,600	9,400
Total agricultural land used for livestock*	14.731m	14.732m
As % of agricultural land	79%	80%
As % of total UK land	60%	60%

* Figures do not include indeterminate land used for potatoes and maize grown as stockfeed (up to about 25,000ha) nor the 64,000ha lying fallow.[3]

In the following chapters on farmed animals, many figures are approximate and most are subject to revision. All 1990 figures are provisional. The main source of figures relating to populations and number of holdings for cattle, sheep, pigs and poultry is *Agriculture in the United Kingdom* (HMSO) and the November or December census. All other information is from sources listed in the **Bibliography**, **Acknowledgements** and **References**.

Population numbers reflect the situation at one specific time of year, e.g. June or December. Slaughter numbers show annual figures totalled.

FARMED ANIMALS: CATTLE

GENERAL: BEEF & DAIRY CATTLE

From the ox (*bos*) genus. Asian ancestors from which *Bos primigenius* evolved. Took the form of the Auroch in Europe. Today's cattle possibly more closely descendant from *Bos taurus* (European) and *Bos indicus* (same family as zebu).

1990 population figures[1]
Total cattle and calves 12.06m, including

Beef		Dairy
0.30m	cows in calf	0.32m
0.22m	heifers in calf	0.53m
1.3m	cows and heifers in milk	2.53m

plus total of 82,000 bulls for service

71,100	farms	44,400

1990 output figures[1]

13m litres	milk	14.8b litres

Beef and veal: 0.99m tonnes (dcw)

1990 slaughter figures[1]
Total of 3.5m, including:

1.03m heifers; 1.48m steers; 334,000 young bulls;
18,000 adult bulls; 625,000 cows; 51,000 calves.

Cows usually produce a single calf. Twins are found in about 1 case in 80. (Identical twins often used in scientific research work).

DAIRY CATTLE

Milk production is the largest UK agricultural enterprise in cash terms. 60-75% dairy cattle are produced by pure breeding by artificial insemination (AI). Bulls can sire up to 15-20,000 calves/ year by AI. Friesian-Holstein breeds account for up to 90% of dairy cattle.

Dairy herd replacements: calves kept and reared on farm, or bought in as in-calf or freshly calved cows and heifers.

Breeding

Main breeds (all figures approximate):

Breed	% of dairy type	Milk yield kg/year
Ayrshire	2	4500-5200
Friesian	87	5000-5800
Guernsey	2	3800-4200
Holstein	3	6000-7000*
Jersey	1.5	3700-4100
Shorthorn	0.5	4500-5500

* 100% increase since 1950.

A gradual movement towards higher-yielding breeds of dairy cows, together with further genetic improvements, will mean that, by 2000, annual milk yields per cow will rise by 5.5%, equivalent to an additional 300 to 350 litres.[2]

Bulls are used for breeding from 1 year old, heifers from 15-18 months. 1 bull to 20 or more cows or heifers. Heifer will have first calf at approx. 2 years of age. Most dairy cows are born in autumn-winter (alternatively spring).

Pregnancy (gestation) lasts approx. 9.5 months (278-285 days). Calving—usually in autumn, calf about 25-42kg—in calving box (12-25 m²) or in straw pen. Lactation lasts approx. 10 months (305 days).

6-8 week period between drying off (cow milked irregularly for a few days then not at all; supplementary food, and maybe water, cut off; bulky diet only) and next calving, prior to which the cow is steamed up—fed high % concentrate to boost milk yield. To get heifer or cow in calf again she is mated 2-3 months after each calving. The dairy cow is simultaneously pregnant and lactating for 6-8 months during each cycle.

Some control and synchronization of cycle by use of prostaglandins.

The cow's lactation produces about 25% more milk than a heifer's. Today's cow has been bred to produce 10 times as much milk as her calf would have drunk, had it been left to suckle. Her full udder can weigh up to 50kg. An energy gap appears in early lactation when milk production is greater than appetite and food intake. Weight loss results, leading to the cow 'milking off her back'. Can lead to ketosis (see **Cattle Diseases**, p47).

Calf Rearing
In the wild, the calf would suckle for 6 months. Modern methods:
• *On-farm natural*. Calf gets milk direct from cow (mother or other). Cow suckles single or double calves or, as nurse cow, multiple-suckles, i.e. suckles calves in batches;
• *Artificial*. Calf taken away from the cow immediately (colostrum fed from bucket) or within 4 days and fed separately. Many different methods. Whole milk now too expensive to feed to calves, but used still for e.g. rearing high quality bulls.

Most calves are weaned early, given colostrum for 1-4 days, then milk substitute for 3-5 weeks and on to dry concentrate foods as early as possible, plus hay or straw *ad lib*. Also liquid feeding systems using cold colostrum or acidified milk. Also, automatic feeders for batches of calves. Autumn-born calves go out to grass in spring. Spring-born out to grass in following spring. Growth: 0.5-1kg increase/day. Mortality 10%, mostly in first 3 weeks.

Housing Calves
When housed, calves kept in pens, individually — 1.0-1.8m² each; or in groups — up to 2.5m² each, after weaning.

Feed & Feeding: General
• *Self sufficiency method*. Maximum cheaper bulky feed produced on farm — grass, silage, hay, kale and roots. Lower yields produced at a lower price.

• *Heavy concentrate method* with moderate bulk feed. Higher yields produced at higher cost. High-yielding dairy cow might eat over 5t feed/year. Examples below (but systems differ).

Calves. Fed from bucket or machine. 350ml milk substitute/ calf plus 0.7kg/day concentrate up to 2.5kg at 3 months. Increasing. Water 15-25 litres/day.

6 months -12 months old. 3-6kg hay/day (partly replaced by equivalent foods).1-3kg concentrates/day. Compound foods or home mixtures. Little or no extra feeding when out to grass in spring-summer.

12 months onwards. 4-10kg hay/day, approx. 2-10kg concentrates depending on milk yield and forage eaten. (Large % of concentrates are fed in the milking parlour). As above re grass.

1kg medium quality hay might be replaced by any one of the following: 0.6kg oats or beet pulp; 0.75kg dried grass or good hay; 3kg silage; 3kg fodder beet or potatoes; 4kg kale, beet tops or swedes; 5kg mangels or wet beet pulp; 0.5kg straw and 3kg kale, beet tops or swedes.[2] Generally 1.5-2.0t concentrates/cow/year.

In addition, secret field trials of the genetically-engineered bovine growth hormone BST (bovine somatotropin) have been taking place on some UK farms with the milk going into the national milk supply unlabelled. BST can increase milk output by up to 14%. Regular injections of BST into the dairy cow can leave swellings; force cow to eat more; become more prone to disease like mastitis. (And see **FARMED ANIMALS: BREEDING & FEEDING** and **VIVISECTION** chapters).

Water. A dairy cow needs 22-100 litres/day. A cow in milk may need up to 3 litres of water/each litre of milk being produced. (Average 70 litres water). Depends on how much dry matter fed. FCR 3.0 (Milk).

Housing

Spring and summer months on pasture; 3-6 cows/ha. Most cows are housed during winter in yards, cowsheds; cows tied in standings. Loose housing or cubicles: 2-2.30m x 1-1.2m. Sawdust, woodshavings, straw. When on slats: 3-4m² /cow. Strawyards: 5m²/cow. 16-hour daylight. Temperature usually uncontrolled. Adult bulls, when inside, sleeping area approx. 16m².

Milking

Mechanized milking parlour (twice, three times/day). Milk extracted by vacuum and pulsation. Uniformity of cow shape and size is demanded to suit the equipment.

Slaughter

Transported by lorry. Up to 15h+ without food/water. Dairy cows are slaughtered at 4-7 years due to disease (36%), poor yield (28%), inability to calve (36%). About 25% are killed before reaching 3-4 years of age. Often pregnant when slaughtered. Meat goes for soup, burgers, processed foods. Mature weight Friesians 660kg, others lighter.

Male calves reared for veal (and see **BEEF CATTLE**). About 10% are killed after a few days for 'bobby' veal or reared for 4 months and killed for quality veal. About 300,000/year are exported live for Continent rearing (often veal crated) and/or slaughter (and see **Appendix C: EXPORT-IMPORT**).

20-25% of dairy herd calves are reared as herd replacements. Most of the rest — bulls, steers, heifers — are reared for prime beef; killed at 1-2 years (and see **BEEF CATTLE**). Natural life expectancy would be 20 years.

BEEF CATTLE

Consult in conjunction with **DAIRY CATTLE** section due to the interrelatedness of dairy and beef industries. 60-75% of beef in UK (except Scotland where 70% of beef is from beef herds) originates from the dairy herd.

Breeding

Mostly cross-breeding, using beef bulls — Hereford, Charolais, Aberdeen Angus, Limousin — (by AI or natural) on dairy cows, usually lower yielders. Beef-type calves from the dairy herd (Friesians) are used to produce intensive young beef. Also, beef cattle from pure-bred beef herds and cross-breeds (with dairy cows), are reared and fattened.

Breeds such as Belgian Blue became popular but due to genetic manipulation these often have to give birth by Caesarian section.

Beef animals are fed to slaughter weight on the one farm or reared on some farms and sold for finishing by others.

Many different systems and much long- and short-distance movement of cattle.

Housing

When not out on grass at 4-10 cattle/ha, adult non-lactating cows and growers over 6 months are kept on slatted or concrete floors. 1.4-2.5m²/cow. 20-25 cows/pen. Cubicles 2 x 1 m. Fattening cattle and beef cows 1.5-4 m². Straw yards: 2-3.5m²at 12 months. 4.5-6m² over 12 months. 10-20 in group. Temperature 2-20°C.

Feeding

Fed a variety of foods; hay, root crops, silage, barley, fishmeal, poultry manure. Plus antibiotics.

Grazing. During spring-summer, grass can provide all or most maintenance and steady growth needs. Can also, with other bulky foods, e.g. up to about 18kg silage/day, fatten beef cattle. Concentrates generally used in addition for fattening, 2-4kg/day.

Young beef. Ration more concentrated, fed *ad lib*. 4kg+ concentrates/day. Plus some straw, silage.

General figures. Cereal beef: 1.6t concentrates/year; 4.7kg feed/kg weight gain. FCR 4-10.0. Water: 25-45 litres/day.

Rearing & Slaughter (and see **DAIRY CATTLE: Slaughter**)
The British government implemented a ban on hormone growth
promoters from 1 December 1986. (Clenbuterol, a beta-antago-
nist, used illegally as growth-promoter in N. Ireland).[4]

• *Veal*. Calf meat. About 3-5 months old, specially reared, grown
quickly and fed on reconstituted milk powder. Straw yards or
pens, in groups. 118-200kg liveweight, deadweight is 60% of this.
Little veal production in UK: about 10,000 calves. The veal crate
was banned in UK from 1990. Other calves are killed within 2
weeks for pies and calf-skin, and rennet from the stomach for
cheese-making.

• *Intensive Beef*. About 20% of British beef. Permanently indoors.
Often from specialist contract-rearing units where calves are
early-weaned off milk replacers at 5 weeks. Mainly Friesian. Production of young, lean beef animals weighing up to 450kg
liveweight, 10-15 months old. Increasingly, animals housed in
pens without bedding, on concrete or slats. Cereal feed.

• *Semi intensive beef*. Hereford x Friesian. Moved from farm of
origin to spend first summer on pasture; finished in yards at end
of second winter (winter finishing) or after second summer at
grass (summer finishing). As with intensive but to a heavier
weight over longer period. 1.25-2 years old, up to 600kg liveweight.

• *Suckler herd*. Up to about 40% of British beef. Calves born in beef
herd (usually spring). Stay with mothers until weaning (230-
290kg: 7-10 months old). Sold or into yards for winter and finished
spring-summer.

• *Traditional Beef*. Hereford x Friesian or Friesian bull calves. 'Store
cattle' — animals reared on one or more farms then sold on. Much
movement from one farm or area to another. Bought for finishing
on grass or in yards — up to 2.5 years old, finished quickly and
cheaply. Up to 700kg liveweight.

Heavier animals usually only for catering trade and processing.

Surgical (Cattle generally)
Disbudding. At 1-3+ weeks. To avoid damage to people and other
stock; allows indoor cattle to be stocked more densely. Achieved
by breeding or by hot iron (anaesthetic should be used). Can be
performed without vet or anaesthetic in first week by chemical

cauterization. Or by hot air. Often performed at same time as...

Castration. Most male calves castrated, if they are not to be kept for bull rearing: by rubber ring in first week of life (no legal requirement for vet or anaesthetic); by the knife — surgical removal of testicles; or bloodless — using Burdizzo emasculators. (Up to 2 months, no legal requirement for vet or anaesthetic).

Marking. 1-2 weeks. Ear tattoo or ear tag. Removing extra teats —snipped off with scissors during first month of life.

Cattle Diseases, Troubles. Beef & Dairy (* = notifiable).

Foot & mouth*, anthrax*, TB (* certain forms), warble fly*, brucellosis*, leucosis*.

Mastitis. Commonest disease of dairy cows — affecting approx. 30% — often caused by dirty methods, bad management, damage. Often contagious. 17m shots of antibiotics are administered to cows' teats/year. Summer mastitis can affect cows between lactations.

Laminitis. Inflammation of foot. Indirectly caused by build up of acid in the rumen via intensive feeding (quick fermenting) concentrates instead of forages like grass, hay, silage. Affects approx 25%. General lameness.

Virus pneumonia (especially in calves: where many kept together, badly ventilated, poor conditions, poor management).

Scours (caused by bacteria, wrong feeding, bad management, too much travelling).*E. coli* infection, leading to septicaemia. Rotavirus, leading to enteritis. Salmonellosis. Shipping fever. Endometritis (inflammation of uterus). Acidosis (digestive disorder caused by large amounts of concentrates in feed). Bloat. Ketosis (acetonaemia: in high-yielding dairy cows after calving). Milk fever (a complaint of high-yielding cows a few days after calving, caused by shortage of calcium in bloodstream). Hypomagnesaemia (grass staggers, grass tetany: shortage of magnesium in bloodstream). Leptospirosis. BVD (mucosal disease). Cryptosporidiosis. Lice and mange. Ringworm. Worms in stomach and intestines. Liver fluke (45% of cattle affected in certain areas). Husk (caused by lungworm).

(And see **Appendix B: BSE**).

2.3

FARMED ANIMALS: DEER

(See also **COUNTRY SPORTS** chapter).

General

Newly domesticated, semi-wild and wild. 3 kinds are farmed in the UK: red deer (80-90%), fallow deer, wapiti-cross.

Deer on farms: approx. 35,000. Approx. 300 deer farms in UK. Typical new deer farm unit averages 100 hinds.

Many farms use hinds taken from the wild. The present system is mainly based on weaned male calves (4-5 months) born on highland farms, transferred as stores in autumn to lowland farms for feeding on to slaughter for venison.

Steady increase in units solely finishing calves for slaughter. Alternatively, yearlings sold at 14-16 months: females for breeding, stags for venison.

Different market from that for venison from wild deer shot on the hill.

Breeding

Hinds and stags are bred from 15-18 months. 1-3 stags to 20-40 hinds. Hinds first calving is at about 2 years.

Heat period (mating season-rut) in September, when stags have shed velvet, and hardened antlers. Oestrus every 18 days. Stags might be changed every 3 weeks. Stags withdrawn from hinds Nov-December. Pregnancy lasts 230-235 days. Calves born late May-June. Fallow and red deer average 1 calf at 6.5-9.5kg.

Embryo transfer and AI on the increase. Hormonal manipulation of breeding times and research into control via melatonin injection to advance the breeding season to move away from virtually all venison being marketed September-Christmas, and avoid costs of over-wintering.

Rearing Young

(In the wild, the hind suckles calf for 6-8 months, calf staying with hind until following autumn).

Colostrum from dams. Hind lactation: 1.1-2.2kg/month; can continue for up to 8 months. Calves suckled for about 4 months or artificially reared (usually the late-born); first 5-8 weeks receiving liquid food (e.g. sheep or goat milk substitute) plus compound.

Usually weaned in September (at about 100 days at 30-50kg), before rut; grazed with supplement concentrate ration, then housed for winter. 10-15% mortality, heaviest just after weaning.

Housing

Outdoors. Fenced enclosures and paddocks. Approx. 5-16 hinds and followers/ha. 15-22 yearling stags/ha (or denser) or on hill range. Breeding adults are usually out-wintered, separately.

Indoors. Groups of 10-15 calves. Housed mature stags (3 years and over) penned individually. Cattle- or sheep-style housing. Floors partially bedded. Weaned calves 1.5-2.25m². Adults 3m².

Surgical

Castration of males not used for breeding. Antlers removed above pedicle when out of velvet, prior to rut and removed for transporting. Dart gun used to immobilize stag. Ear tagging. Feet trimming.

Feed

Grazing and browsing, heather, plus supplementation — concentrates and hay.

If housed for winter, hind calves are fed high protein (barley and fishmeal-based) concentrate until turned out in April-May. Up to 1.45kg/day plus hay *ad lib* — 0.33-1.28kg/day.

Pregnant hinds over winter, approx. equivalent of 10kg/day silage or 0.5kg/day concentrate. Stags approx. equivalent of 12.5kg roots/day; 1.25-3kg/day concentrate over winter indoors. Stag calves: ration reduced during mid-winter inappetance — grass, hay, silage, kale, roots.

Outdoors: grass, silage, hay, straw, dairy nuts, concentrate.

General: stags and hinds 40kg concentrate/year each; hind over winter (175 days) 66kg hay. FCR approx. 2.0-5.0.

Diseases, Problems (* = notifiable)

Tuberculosis*. Anthrax*. Salmonellosis. Catarrhal fever. Deer Herpes. Toxoplasmosis. Intestinal worms. Scours. Dystocia. Clostridial disease. Crytosporidiosis. Liver fluke. Warble fly. Nasal bot fly. Acidosis. Undernutrition. Lung worm. Catarrhal fever.

Slaughter

Approx 10,000/year. Usually at 13-27 months; 60-75kg. (Fallow deer about half this weight). Breeding females at 12-15 years, stags at 5-8 years — at 80-115kg. Natural life expectancy 17 years.

Slaughterhouse. Transported in special or conventional cattle trucks. Normally slaughtered separately from other species. Stunned by captive bolt or free bullet, stuck and bled. Slaughterhouse figures. 1987: 880. 1988: 430. (Deer in velvet cannot be transported to or put through slaughterhouse. Yearling stags are in velvet May-July).

Or killed on farm (most). Stunned by captive bolt in handling crate or shot by rifle, stuck and bled. Rifle: frontal head shot from 10-20m. High neck shot to break spinal cord from 40m. Groups of up to 10 taken at a time.

Approx. 500t farmed venison produced/year. (Approx. 3,000t venison is produced from the wild deer shoot).

2.4

FARMED ANIMALS: GOATS

General

75-150,000 goats are used in the UK for milk or fibre. Approx. 8,000 are used for mohair (about 600 holdings); 1,500 for cashmere (about 10-20 holdings), in herds of 50-200 does. Fibre annual output approx. 25t mohair; 155kg cashmere.[1]

The majority of goats are kept on smallholdings. Average dairy herd size 9-10. Less than 1% consist of over 100. Largest dairy unit approx. 500.

Very few are reared specifically for meat, which is regarded as a by-product of dairy and fibre herds. All numbers increasing.

Breeds

• *Milk* — British Saanen, British Toggenburg, British Alpine (all Swiss origin) used for more intensive milk production; Anglo Nubian (from Middle and Far East) for milk quality.

• *Mohair* — Angora (Turkey origin, but imported from New Zealand, Canada, Tasmania and USA);

• *Cashmere* — Indigenous feral (W. & N. Scotland) goats crossed with bloodlines from Iceland, NZ, Tasmania and Siberia.

Breeding

Artificial insemination, superovulation and embryo transfer increasingly used on breeding stock.

Males (bucks) used as from about 18 months. 1 male to 30-50 or more females. Females (does) are in heat for 1-2 days at 21-day intervals during August-February. Usually mated in first or second autumn from 6-18 months old and then annually.

Out of season breeding practised especially in dairy herds, via use of intra-vaginal progesterone-impregnated pessaries (includes use of prostaglandin injections and PMSG dose); and use of artificially extended daylight, up to 20 hours out of 24, during winter.

Gestation 146-156 days, average 150 days. Females kid once/ year, sometimes twice, producing single kids, twins or triplets, weighing 2-5kg/kid. Mean litter size in UK is 1.75. (Goatlings usually have just one kid. Anglo Nubian litters up to 4+.).

• *Dairy goats*. Lactation (2 teats) ordinarily lasts 10 months. In dairy herds it is usual to give a 2 month dry period before kidding. Yield will rise again in spring — with fall in oestrogen level — in females not mated in the autumn. Many goats lactate continuously for 2-4 years or more. Dam stripped out twice/day to stop milk decreasing. Kids separated from mothers after 1-4 days (after receiving colostrum), reared on calf, lamb or goat milk replacers. Weaned off replacers at 6-10 weeks. Females used for breeding and milk. Dairy herd females valuable, and some males for breeding. Other male kids culled.

• *Fibre herds*. Males and females produce fibre. Kids run in suckler herd until weaned at 12-14 weeks. Kids may be put to a dairy goat so fibre doe can be put back to buck to become pregnant again to produce 2 litters of kids/year. Kids thus reared grow quicker and can be mated earlier. Approx. 25% of female kids are kept as herd replacements, others are sold.

Other kids sold off at markets, many whilst still unweaned.

Housing

Outdoors. Usually rudimentary, floored shelter from sun and rain. Cashmere goats are reared more often under hill farm conditions with little, often only natural shelter, or moveable shelters holding 20-30 goats, 0.5-0.75m²/goat. Fibre herds up to 25/ha.

Indoors. Open-sided housing and various others once used for other farm species. Straw, sawdust, wood shavings or slatted floor. Often individually stalled: 0.9-1.5m². Dairy kids penned in groups of approx. 12+, with 0.5-1.5 m² floor space each. Single housing, 2.0-2.5m². Breeding males in blockbuilt pens up to 3m². Fibre goats indoors after shearing.

Production

• *Milk*. Approx. 500-2000 litres milk/goat/year. Milked by hand, or by machine in larger herds. Once or twice/day.

• *Mohair*. Single coat, continuous growth from Angora goat. (NB.

Mohair is different to Angora wool from Angora rabbits). 1.5-10kg/goat/year; highest from bucks and wethers. Sheared every 6 months, just before mating in autumn and before kidding in spring. Herds can contain a high number of wethers sold for meat at a later age. Other farmers take one or two shearings from kids not required for herd replacement, before slaughter for meat.

•*Cashmere* (fine undercoat). Crossbred feral goats. Seasonal growth, shed in late winter-early spring. Fibre removed by combing 1-3 times during Dec-May or by shearing: de-haired cashmere is about 25% of the clip. Goat will take 8-10 weeks to grow new coat. Annual yield up to about 250g/goat. Harvested from adult breeding stock, and from previous season's kids at 10-12 months who are then sold for slaughter or kept for 6 more months. Scotland is the largest processor of cashmere.

• *Meat*. Mostly from castrated male kids, surplus to requirements, and cull does. FCR 5.0.

Surgical

Castration of males not required for breeding; rubber ring method in first week or by knife. After 2 months, by vet and anaesthetic.

Disbudding; in first 10 days by red hot iron. (Dehorning adult goat to be avoided). Both by vet and anaesthetic.Ear tatooing, marking. Freeze branding. Deodorization; red hot iron to musk glands at base of horn (anaesthetic). Hoof trimming.

Feeding

Fibre goats are fed similarly to sheep. Browsing. Leaves, small branches, hay, silage, chopped roots, sugar beet pulp, kale, mangolds. When housed, mainly hay and silage and sugar beet pulp.

Milk herds. Milkers often considered as scaled down dairy cows re nutrition. Non-lactating females: forage *ad lib*. Pregnant animals: forage *ad lib* plus 250g-450g dairy concentrate/day in last 2 months. Lactating animals: forage *ad lib* plus 1.5-1.8kg concentrates. Kids onto concentrates at about 3 weeks. FCR 5-9.0.

Water. 2.5 litres/day plus 4 x quantity of milk produced, up to average of 4-7 litres/day. Thirst often stimulated by adding salt to water to increase milk yield.

Diseases, Problems

Mastitis. Stress. Lameness. Scald. Foot rot. Clostridial diseases: enterotoxaemia; pulpy-kidney; tetanus. Pneumonia. Louping ill (virus can be secreted in the milk). Johne's disease. Acetonaemia. Blindness. Orf. Pregnancy toxaemia. Caprine arthritis encephalitis. Hypocalcaemia (milk fever). Hypomagnesaemia. Bloat. Scurvy. Bladder stones. Parasitic gastro-enteritis. Lungworm. Coccidiosis. Liver fluke. Lice. Mange. Ticks. Pizzle rot.

Slaughter

Milking goats at 6-8 years old (natural life expectancy over 15 years), at 30-100kg depending on sex and breed. Fibre goats: some at 9 months after first clip; others after second clip. Plus cull does and bucks.

Slaughter by vet, by (commonly halal) slaughterhouse or slaughterhouse personnel. Stunned, bled out. Meat for restaurants, private customers.

Kids not required are often killed on farm at birth or within 4 days, by overdose of barbiturates or by chloroform or stunned and bled out. Others, 3-16 weeks, sold, given away.

2.5

FARMED ANIMALS: PIGS

General

Naturally forest animals, derived from wild boar with some Chinese crossing.

About 50% of all meat eaten in the world comes from pigs. About 33.3% of meat eaten in the UK is pig meat.

1990 figures: total UK population of 7.4m, including 0.66m sows in-pig, and others for breeding; 0.97 gilts in-pig; 43,000 boars for service. 12,500 breeding farms; 12,200 fattening farms.

Breeding

Pure breeding: landrace, large white and Welsh breeds, and crossbreeding (70-75%): White boar on other sows . Other breeds used: Hampshire, Duroc, saddleback. Main white breeds are often crossed together. Average number of piglets in litter is 12 (8-10 surviving). Largest litters come from sows served more than once when mated.

Boars (male pigs) are used for breeding from 5-9 months. Usually bought in from specialized breeders. 'Natural' mating: one boar for up to 20-25 sows. Sows often tethered in rack for the purpose. Artificial insemination used as alternative to natural mating, in 5-10% of UK services.

Gilts (young female pigs) are mated from about 6-8 months old at 90-110kg. On heat every 21 days until 'in pig'. Most gilts are flushed prior to mating. Heat period lasts 2-3 days. First heat (and usually next mating) after birth of a litter usually comes 3-7 days after the litter is weaned but depends on suckling period. (Natural breeding season autumn-June).

The sow (female pig after first litter) or gilt is in pig for about 115 days. Farrowing time is often induced by prostaglandin injection, progesterone dose and/or gonadotrophin hormone.

Piglets weigh about 1.3kg at birth, 10-20% dying before weaning, mostly in first 2-4 days of life. Average weight at 3 weeks is 5.5kg. At 8 weeks 18kg.

Sow or gilt suckles — 14 teats —her litter for 3-5 weeks*. (8-12 weeks in the wild). Very early weaning, before 14 days, sometimes practised, to get sow to farrow as often as possible. After weaning, piglets removed to grower accommodation, and sows back to dry sow stalls for re-mating as soon as possible (7-28 days).

At least 66% of a sow's life is spent pregnant. Average breeding life: 2-2.5 litters/year. 22-25 pigs reared/sow/year is the aim. Sow will produce 5-7 litters, then, at average of 4 years of age, be slaughtered for sausages etc. Natural life span 15-20 years.

Housing

As many systems as there are farmers but pig production is mainly (80-90%) indoors. All figures approximate.

• *Boars*. Pens. 7.2-12m² (incl. lying area). In sight of sows.

• *Dry (in-pig) sows*. Mostly tubular steel-frame stalls 1.3 x 0.6-1.0m/sow, side by side on concrete or slatted floors, tied either by neck or with strap round girth. Fed in troughs, not allowed out for exercise, cannot turn. Over 400,000 (up to 60% of total) sows spend most of their lives thus. Temperature approx. 14-20°C. Close confinement stalls and tethering to be banned as from 1.1.99. Others in yards, in groups of 20-40 (2.7 x 3.7m/sow); or pens 2.1 x 1.5m/sow.

• *Farrowing crates*. Sows put here in rows of crates 3-7 days before ready to farrow (give birth). Metal crate 2.4 x 0.6m, concrete or metal-grid floor. Remain lying or standing on floor for 3-5 weeks, unable to exercise, suckling piglets. Before weaning, piglets allowed warmer creep area, 0.1m²/piglet. Temp. approx. 24-30°C. 12-14 hr 'daylight'.

Early-weaned piglets (taken from mothers 2-3 weeks, sometimes at one day old) often kept for 2-10 weeks up to 15kg on the wire mesh of tiered cages in darkened building. Cages of 8 piglets; 0.15m²/piglet. Temp. 28°C.

Others in flat decks, metal slatted floor (0.15-0.25m²/pig. Groups of 10-20) or verandah type housing with outside dunging area. Strawed yards 0.5 m²/pig. Temp. approx. 23-27°C.

• *Fattening pigs*. From 10 weeks to slaughtering, housed in yards but more commonly inside in darkness or low light, often in boxed pens with concrete walls and floor with slatted drainage area or entirely slatted. Pigs crowded, no bedding straw. 10-40 pigs/pen. 0.5-1.5 m²/pig.

Some pigs in sweat boxes. Totally closed housing, each unit of about 20 pigs, tightly stocked. Minimum ventilation, high 'natural' temperature and humidity.

Young boars group-housed in straw yards.

• *Outdoor system*. Approx. 10-15% of national herd. Herds of up to 1,000 sows at 10-15 sows/ha. Piglets weaned at 3-4 weeks and transferred indoors. Sows fed slightly more than if indoors and sometimes tethered. Half-round timber-framed huts; solid back and roofed to ground with corrugated iron. Used for dry and farrowing sows. Greater use of saddleback x sows.

Surgical

Piglets' sharp incisor teeth are usually nipped off with pliers within 24 hours of birth.

Castration of about 10% of all piglets reared for slaughter, by farmer or vet. (To avoid boar taint, despite pigs now being slaughtered below the weight where this applies.) Commonly at 1-10 days old (sometimes up to 3 weeks) by skin incision; Elastrator in first week. Castration after 2 months by vet + anaesthetic.

Taildocking. Routinely performed in first few days of life to prevent tail-biting in fattening pigs. After 7 days by vet + anaesthetic. Leaves short stump. Ear-notching. Ear tagging. Tattooing.

Castration, ear-notching and taildocking might all be performed together within 48 hours of birth.

Feeding

Pig's small stomach and simple digestive system is unable to cope with heavy bulk or fibre content. Fed on mainly ready-mixed compounds of concentrated grains and protein foods. Often mixed on farm, possibly with small amounts of green foods or roots. Unless pregnant or lactating, breeding sows are kept hungry to prevent weight gain. Dried skim milk often included in 2-4 week weaned piglet diet.

Average daily rations: at 3-week weaning 100-150g/day. Piglets injected with iron within 48 hours of birth. Young breeding stock: 1.4 - 2.7kg. Pregnant sow: 1.8-3.6kg (670gm/50kg liveweight). Lactating sow: 4-8kg. Full grown boar: 3-5kg. Fattening Pigs: 0.9-2.7kg (113gm/week of age/day).

Water. 3.5 litres/day at 8 weeks; 7-9 litres at 6 months. A boar, or a sow in milk, may need up to 22-30 litres/day. FCR 3.0-5.0.

Pig Diseases, Troubles (* = notifiable)

Foot & mouth*. Aujeszky's disease*. Anthrax*. Teschen disease*. Swine vesicular disease*. Swine erysipelas (diamonds). Blue Ear. Swine fever. Virus pneumonia. Enteritis. Anaemia. Oedema (stress-related). Lameness affects approx. 10-15%. *E. coli*, mastitis, metritis, agantia, arthritic and rheumatoid conditions. Lice. Mange. Roundworms. Lungworms. Skin abrasions. Stereotypic behaviour.

Young pigs reared under indoor conditions are prone to piglet anaemia, shown by scouring, weakness and paleness.

Production, Growth, Slaughter

Specialized production. Farmers breed only, fatten only or breed and fatten.

• *Young pigs.* Some farmers breed only and sell the young pigs through markets or direct as weaners (5-8 weeks; 18-35kg) or as stores (10-12 weeks) for finishing.

• *Pork.* Pigmeat sold fresh. Lightweight about 60kg; heavy or cutters 80kg. Average pork weight is 70kg. 4-5 months old.

• *Bacon.* Pigmeat cured in factory. Sold 'green' or smoked. Average 90kg liveweight. 5-7 months old.

• *Manufacturing (heavy pigs).* Heavy and cull pigs. Average liveweight 110kg. 5-7 months old.

Breeding boars killed after 2-4 years. Breeding sows killed at 2-6 years. Gilts failing to come on heat by 8 months, killed. Natural life expectancy 15-20 years.

1990 slaughter figures: 322,000 sows and adult boars; 13.9m fattened pigs.

Meat may be pale, soft and exudative (PSE) or dark, firm and dry (DFD) from poor handling.

Swill Pigs[2]

Swill is almost anything that was once edible. Cheap. Until 1973 there were virtually no controls on swill. The Diseases of Animals (Waste Food) Order 1973 followed a severe outbreak of swine vesicular disease which ravaged the UK pig population. Permitted items of refuse include any discarded 'meat bones, blood, offal, or other part of the carcase of any livestock or of any poultry or product derived therefrom or hatchery waste or eggs or egg shells.' Hatchery waste means dead chicks, faeces and feathers.

The 1973 Order requires a red cross to be painted on all swill pigs to ensure the pigs go straight to slaughterhouse and then to butchers shops.

Before the Order there were more than 4,000 swine swill farms. The number of licensed operators fell to 1,300 by 1987. Today, according to the MAFF, there are 312 licensed operators. Poor conditions.

MAFF appoints veterinary inspectors to control swill farms and visits are said to occur up to 4 times a year, but it's customary to warn farm before inspection. In 1988 there were 17 prosecutions in England and Wales. In 1989 there were 4.

FARMED ANIMALS: POULTRY

HENS & CHICKENS: General

To speed up maturity, growth and production, day length is routinely manipulated in poultry houses during brooding, rearing and production periods. Daylight = low light, to minimize featherpecking and cannibalism.

Hatchery waste is macerated to kill living embryos. Unwanted poults are disposed of by gassing with CO_2, by neck dislocation, by suffocation, by drowning or by decapitation. In the case of laying stock, 35-50m 'day old' (up to 72 hours old) males/year are thus slaughtered and used for fertilizer.

Over 0.5m were compulsorily slaughtered in 1990 due to salmonella.

Layers and broilers are bred for separate, specific purposes.

Layers

Descended from red jungle fowl. (In the wild, annual breeding; approx. 12-24 eggs/year).

1990 UK population figures: 33.4m plus 10.4m pre-lay pullets. Approx. 7m in layer and broiler breeding flocks. 33,8000 layer farms but only about 1,000 hold over 5,000 each.[1]

Breeding

7-10 males to 100 hens. AI often used instead. Eggs into incubators. Hatching females vaccinated and possibly debeaked and decombed in first 10 days. (Males: see above). Chicks sent in boxes from hatcheries on (up to) 24 hr trips to farms or laying units. Unfertilized and late-hatched eggs are macerated. Chicks are supplied to the laying industry by about 6 companies.

Chicks are reared on deep litter at about $0.72m^2/20$ birds at 18 weeks (transferred to battery cages at approx. 16-18 weeks) or in cages straight off.

Output

Output is approx. 920m dozen eggs/year. Each bird lays an average of 5 eggs/week, beginning at about 18-20 weeks of age. Will be slaughtered at 1-2 years of age, usually at 12-15 months, after first moult. Some are pushed into second laying period after a moult forced by food and water deprivation (this now illegal) and a sharp contrast in lighting conditions which regulate the pituitary gland's influence on laying pattern.

(Pulled) eggs are often removed from dead hens. Hen in second year of lay produces larger eggs.

Housing

80-90% of British eggs are taken from hens kept 4 or 5 to a 50 x 45cm wire cage — each bird has wingspan of approx. 80cm — (each bird having 450-460cm². space in the cage). Each hen must have 10 cm of feed trough and continuous drink channel or two nipple-drinkers/cage. Minimum height of 40cm over 65% of cage, and floor slope not more than 8° (all cages as from 1995). Sloping wire floor. No allowance for perching, ground scratching, dustbathing, exercise, nest-egg-laying.

Each bank of cages reaches up to 6-8 tiers high. Tens of thousands of birds are often held in one windowless building. Automatic feeding, watering, ventilation and egg-collection.

Other systems (2-4m birds):

• *Free Range*. Littered, movable sheds. Daytime access to open- air runs; maximum of 1,000 birds/ha (one bird /10 m²). Traditional free range density was approx. 360/ha. Interior of house, now a minimum of 400cm²/bird, and 15cm perch space;

• *Semi-intensive*. Deep litter system with outdoor run. Max. 4,000 hens/ha (one bird/2.5m²), and as above;

• *Straw Yards*. As for deep litter but 4-7 hens/m². Housed at end of summer. Manual feeding and egg-collection. Daylight manipulation;

• *Deep Litter*. Indoor housing. One third of floor covered in litter — straw, wood shavings, sand or turf. 7 hens/m². Often used for breeding flocks.

• *Aviary*. Decks of slatted-floor perches. Approx 12 birds/m² floor

space. Nesting boxes. Food, water, egg-collection automated. Lighting manipulated;
• *Perchery (Barn)*. Indoor housing with 3-5 tiers or perches. Wire floor, droppings-pit below. 25 hens/m² floor space plus 15cm perch space/hen.

Surgical
Debeaking performed (on approx. 30%) in attempt to stop feather-pecking, on chicks of 0-10 days old, and/or at 6-8 weeks or later if aggression is a problem. Red-hot blade. Can affect feeding and cause shock and death. Decombing or dubbing: within 72 hours, by scissors; older birds by vet. Toe cutting: within 72 hours; by vet thereafter. Dewinging: flight feathers of one wing clipped.

Feed
Feed accounts for 70% of egg production costs. *Ad lib* feeding of ready mixed (or farm mixed) compound food in meal or pellet form. Contains cereals mixed with high quality (15-18% protein) foods, minerals and vitamins.

The average modern hybrid hen eats up to 50kg food/year (85-140g/day) highly concentrated foods. National flock consumes up to 2m tonnes/year. Can include dried milk, yeast, liver meal and seeds. Typical compound includes antibiotics and coccidiostats, plus pigments to colour yolks.

It takes approx. 670kg of feed protein to produce 180kg of egg protein (27% efficiency) and 20kcal of feed energy plus 13 kcal of fossil fuel energy to produce 1 kcal of egg protein.[2] Other sources show 18% protein conversion rate. Average FCR 2.5-5.0.

Water. National flock drinks up to 10m litres/day (0.25 litre/day/bird).

Diseases, Problems (mostly due to intensive conditions).
Loss of feathers; brittle and broken bones; fatty liver syndrome; psychosis; salmonella. Aggression; feather-pecking; head-flicking; vacuum dust-bathing; hysteria; cannibalism. Enteric diseases. Respiratory. Degenerative. Egg peritonitis. Ascites (body fluids; tumours in abdominal cavity). Tumours (tumours of oviduct have increased with increased egg-laying volume). Viral

cancer. Newcastle disease. Marek's disease. Leucosis.

Soil-borne diseases in free range systems. Coccidiosis. Round worms, tapeworms. Prolapses. Gumboro disease. Salmonella.

Approx 6% (2m) mortality.

Slaughter

At 1-2 years (natural life expectancy 5-10 years) for soups, pastes, stock cubes and baby foods. Grabbed by gangs of catchers and loaded into crates on lorry for transporting — exposed to the elements on long trips — to slaughterhouse-processing plant. Often long delays. Approx. 25% suffer broken bones as a result of handling and transport.

Only about 6 major processing-slaughter plants in UK take end-of-lay hens.

Broilers

Breeding

1990 population 73.4m on 1,900 farms.[1] Mainly hybrids derived from white rock and Cornish game breeds. Most supplied by specialist hatcheries to farms at a day old. Major companies breed, hatch, grow, feed and process.

Approx. 6m birds are kept in parent stock, mostly on deep litter. Some caged and artificially inseminated. Approx. 10 hens to one cockerel. Chick production: 115-130/hen in 60 weeks. Kept for approx. 64 weeks then slaughtered at about 4kg. Around 2.5% are mini-mums, specially bred to be half size.

38% of males and 6% of females are culled over first 24 weeks. From 24 weeks until slaughter, mortality and culling run at 10-15% for males and 6% for females. Kept hungry.

Housing

Pullets and cockerels are often housed separately due to different growth rates. Reared in tens of thousands in windowless sheds — containing up to 100,000 birds (average 20-30,000) — artificially dimly lit for 23.5 hours out of 24 (half-hour darkness) with often only one person responsible. First 3 days brightly lit. Alternatively, intermittent daylight.

Loose on floor on wood shavings (not changed in 6-7 week life-time of each group of birds). Stocking density 0.1-0.2 m²/bird (27-34kg/m²). Some de-beaked. Temp. 18-24°C.

Approx 5-6 'crops' of birds/year/rearing shed.

Feed

Fed *ad lib* on starter crumbs then pellets. 0.2-0.4kg/bird/day. Includes antibiotics serving also as growth promoters at approx. rate of 20g/t of feed for 4 weeks out of the 7-week life. Anticoccidial drugs.

A 7-week old, 2.1kg broiler will have eaten about 4.25kg feed by time of slaughter. FCR: (range = 2.0-10.0). Water: each bird approx. 0.5 litres/day. National flock approx. 300m litres/day.

Diseases, Problems

Ammonia, excrement-ridden floor causes burns on legs and breasts, and ulcerated feet. Leg and feet deformities.

Salmonella. Campylobacter (breeding ground is litter in sheds as above). Listeria. Respiratory disease. Heart attacks (acute death syndrome), fatty liver, kidney syndrome, colisepticaemia, Marek's disease (form of cancer).

Stunting syndrome. Dehydration. Emaciation. Keratoconjunctivitis. Perosis. Staphylococcal arthritis. Gumboro disease (aka chicken AIDS). Botulism. Newcastle disease.

Mortality. 20-36m birds (approx. 6%) die annually in the sheds before reaching slaughter-age. Common cause, heart attack.

Breeding stock. Reproductive disorders, viral conditions including viral tenosynovitis, leukosis.

Slaughter, Production

Caught at night by gangs. Crated on lorry. Mortality in transit about 1% (5-6m).

607 m broiler (table) chickens — either sex — were slaughtered in 1990 in the UK. Killed when 6-7 weeks old (sexual maturity still 12 weeks away) when hatched weight has been multiplied approx. 60 times to about 1.45-2.75kg. (Twice the weight of a chicken reared 25 years ago).

Roasting birds (capons) 4.0-4.5kg produced by growing on.

Caponization by castration is now illegal in the UK (1981-2).

Spring chicken (poussins) are slaughtered at 26-30 days old at 0.45-1.5kg. Chicken's natural lifespan is 5-10 years.

Total 1990 output: 0.8m tonnes.

Other Systems

EC regulations from 1.7.91 specify 4 grades of free range 'broiler': *extensive indoor* (not really free range) — 12 birds/m², slaughtered at 56 days; *free range* — continuous daytime access to open air, 13 birds/m², slaughtered at 56 days; *traditional free range* — must be different breed to the usual white used as broiler, continuous access to fields, 12 birds/m², slaughtered at 81 days; *free range total freedom* — slow-growing strains, continuous access to unlimited area in open air.

TURKEYS

Originally native of N. America. Domesticated for short period only and thus more sensitive to farming conditions. White-feathered type most common. 1990 UK population 9.4m.

Breeding

Artificial insemination. Modern male breeding turkey is too heavy (around 27kg) to mate. Some are caged; solid floors. Daylight manipulation. Semen 'milked' from males every 2-3 days. Female inseminated by syringe and tube, or by blowing semen through tube, into vagina. First eggs after 32 weeks. Eggs to artificial incubators. Three main strains: traditional farm fresh (TFF); fast-growers; dual purpose. Worn-out breeding turkeys are slaughtered for processing into pies etc.

Housing

Kept on floor litter in pole barns — open-sided, natural light and ventilation — or in broiler sheds — conditions as for broiler chickens but less densely stocked: 0.25-0.5m²/bird. Up to about 15,000/shed. Male-female separation. Lighting manipulated. Temp. 17°C.

Breeding stock. 0.5-1.0 m²/bird; groups of 25-30 in pens, or singly in cages. Males kept for AI: 1 m²/bird.

Surgical

75-80% are debeaked, at 5-7 days old, with secateurs or hot cauterizing blade. Nostrils are often damaged. Birds kept for breeding might be debeaked again at 14-18 weeks. Desnooding: snoods pulled off in 1-21 days; by vet thereafter. Toe cutting: within first 72 hours; by vet thereafter. Dewinging: flight feathers of one wing clipped when reducing effects of flightiness.

Feed

Poults (day-olds) fed in the form of crumbs for first 3-4 weeks. On to pellets or mash. High protein. 0.4-0.6kg/day/bird at 16 weeks. Restricted diet, kept hungry. Ration includes (growth-promoting) antibiotics and anticoccidials.

FCR 2.0-4.0. Water 0.4-0.75 litres/day/bird.

Diseases, Problems

Mortality approx. 5-7%. Many poults die due to 'starve-outs': failure to locate food and water points. Other birds trampled. Foot ulcers. Blepharo conjunctivitis. Breast blisters, ulcers. Colisepticaemia. Blackhead (liver damage). Turkey rhinotracheitis (TRT). Haemorrhagic enteritis. Coccidiosis. Fowl cholera. Newcastle disease. Salmonella. Diseased hip joints. Cannibalism. Pecking.

Breeding stock. Approx. 80% of males suffer lameness through antitrochanteric degeneration.

Slaughter

1990 figure: 33.5m. Aged 12-26 weeks (males at older end of range) at approx. 5.2-7.2kg. Older, catering-size birds and ex-breeders (about 1 year) up to 36kg+ (averaging 12-15kg). Natural lifespan approx. 10 years.

Starved a minimum of 12 hours before slaughter. Caught by gangs of catchers by feet and thrust into crates on lorry, causing skin blemishes, bruising, broken blood vessels. Traditional farm fresh turkeys; 24 hours starvation prior to slaughter.

1990 output 0.16m tonnes.

DUCKS

1990 UK population: 1.85m. Of the 8-10m ducks produced annually in the UK , 70% come from Cherry Valley Farms, Lincs.

Breeding

Two main breeds: Aylesbury and Pekin-mallard. Selected from meat stock at 7 weeks and kept on range, with basic — if any — shelter. 1 drake to 5-8 ducks. Then housed. Daylight up to 20 hrs+. First eggs at approx. 24 weeks of age. Lay for 30-40 weeks.

Natural or forced moult, then second lay. Each lay approx. 140-200 eggs. Culled after 2-3 cycles. Or forced moult every 20 weeks with 10 week lay-offs between. Culled after 3 years.

(Forced moult: artificial lighting eliminated. Starved for 24 hours, then low ration, steadily built up for next cycle).

Eggs incubated (28 days to hatch). After artificial brooding period on wire mesh floor (6-25/m²), ducklings will be moved to rearing house at 3 weeks.

Housing

Variety of buildings and/or range as above. Solid floor: wood shavings, straw (stocking density 8+ birds/m²) or on slatted, perforated or metal mesh floors (stocking density about 7+ birds/m²). Daylight manipulation. Grass pens: 2,500-5000 birds/ha. Traditional: brooding on wire floors or litter then transferred at 3 weeks to grass pens in flocks of 100s. Marketed at 7-8 weeks.

Breeding ducks. Solid floor: 3 birds/m². Slatted, wire-floored etc: 5 birds/m². Natural floor: 1 bird/m². Nest boxes (about 1 to every 3 layers), roosting areas, raised pens. Outside: 4,000/ha.

Surgical

Dewinging. Bills trimmed at 1 week or older by hot blade; front rim of upper bill removed (before birds leave rearer housing). Webs slit for marking. Bands or tags attached to inner wing.

Feeding

Ducks grow faster than other poultry. Compound pellets, high protein. 170-250g/day/bird. Future breeders fed only up to 75% of appetite. Water about 1 litre/day. FCR approx. 3.0.

Diseases, Problems (* = notifiable)

Chlamydiosis*. Duck viral hepatitis (DVH). Enteritis. Salpingitis. Septicaemia. Respiratory disease. Mycotoxicosis. Liver disease. Duck plague. Newcastle disease. Salmonellosis. Coccidiosis. Lameness. Feather-pulling.

Slaughter

1990: 10m. Ducklings approx. 7-8 weeks old at slaughter. Weight about 2.5-3.2kg. Starved for about 6 hours prior to slaughter. Breeding stock at about 3 years. Natural life expectancy 7-10 years. 1990 output: 21,000t.

GEESE

1990 UK population 0.17m. Most popular breeds: Embden, Toulouse, Roman, Chinese and hybrids.

Breeding

One gander pairs (sets) with 3-5 geese. Breeding season usually November. Goose lays 30-75 eggs/year (Feb-June). Lighting manipulation — 6 weeks of short days then back to long — stimulates another cycle. Eggs incubated naturally or artificially — 29-32 days to hatch. 20-25 goslings/goose/season.

Housing

Breeding stock at about 100 birds/ha on short grass and/or in simple buildings on shavings or straw litter with nest boxes, about 2.0m²/bird.

Growers mostly outdoors (night housing) at 125-750 birds/ha. Indoors: 5-17 birds/m². In sheds of about 8,000 birds from day one.

Feeding

Chick pellets for first 3-4 weeks. Mainly grazed and/or penned in straw yards with small concentrate supplements, e.g. 150g/day, then *ad lib* in last 6 weeks.

Breeders 115-225g pelleted ration/day. Fed *ad lib* in laying season. Also waste veg. FCR 2.0-4.0.

Surgical
Toe punching. Leg or wing banding. Bill trimming.

Diseases, Problems
Gizzard worm. Newcastle disease. Salmonellosis. Coccidiosis. Leg deformities. Cannibalism.

Slaughter
1990 figure: 1m. Intensive-raised (no grazing) at 8-12 weeks at 3.4-5.4kg. Others up to 22 weeks at 5.4-7.5kg. Starved for 12 hours before killing. Breeding geese at up to 10 years; ganders at up to 4-5 years. Natural life expectancy 10+ years. 1990 output: 3,000t.

GUINEA FOWL
Mainly small-scale.

Breeding, Housing
Flock-mating: 1 male to 6-10 females, or breeders kept in cages and AI used: 1 male to 3 females. Usually on shavings litter, 8-9 birds/m² with nestboxes. Temp. 25°C. 10-17 hours 'daylight'. 100+ eggs/year from 4.5-9 months onwards.

Keets (young birds) brooded on litter (21 birds/m² in 250-bird groups) or in cages (45 birds/m² in 50-bird groups). 23 hours light. After 6 weeks may be run on range at 1,500/ha. Mortality 5%.

Surgical. De-beaking. One-wing clipping.

Feed. Similar to broilers, *ad lib*. Approx. 100-115g/bird/day. FCR 4-6.0.

Diseases, Problems. Drowning (in drinker). Injury through flightiness. Blackhead. Coccidiosis. *E.coli*. Worms. Salmonella.

Slaughter. At 8-12 weeks at 1.25kg. Breeding females at 2-3 years, males at 1 year. Necks broken.

QUAIL

Breeding stock kept in cages as for battery hens; growers raised as for broilers. Smaller scale. Up to about 10,000 birds/unit. Similar treatment; diseases; troubles etc. Caged layers often injured in attempts to fly.

FARMED ANIMALS: RABBITS

From Mediterranean countries in 12th century. Farm population approx. 5-10m (meat rabbits) on 1,500-2,000 farms. 50-200+ breeding does/farm.

Breeding

Two pure breeds are mainly used for meat production: commercial white (from New Zealand White) — albino more popular, and Californian. Others used: Belgian hare, Flemish giant, giganta, beveren. Mostly bred and fattened on farm. Others bred and supplied to farms for breeding or meat production.

Does of modern strains can rear over 60 young/year. On 17-hour day length, will breed all year.

Does are mated at approx. 5 months of age; bucks from 6 months. One buck to 10-15 does. Matings per buck: 4/day, 12/week. Doe placed in buck's cage. Doe often hand-held in mating position for buck. Little artificial insemination but when done, hormone injected into doe to stimulate ovulation.

Gestation period 29-33 days. Mated again approx. 3-4 weeks after giving birth, but sometimes after 2 weeks or after 3-7 days where full lactation and early pregnancy occur simultaneously. Doe produces 5-10 litters/year. Average number in litter 8-10. Does have 8+ teats, producing up to 140+g/milk/day. Young are weaned at 3-5 weeks (in wild, 6-7 weeks).

Housing

Mostly indoors — cowsheds, barns etc. In flat-deck or tiered wire cages with mesh floors, no bedding. Cages approx. 30-45cm tall. (Or hutches). Floor space approx. 0.50-0.75 m², housing one buck or doe, or doe and litter up to 4 weeks, or 5-8 growers up to 10 weeks (slaughter). Stud bucks and breeding does are caged or hutched individually.

Open-topped wooden, plastic or cardboard nesting box — about 40 x 25-30 x 25-30cm (front 10-15cm high) —is placed with hay or shavings in cage of pregnant doe for parturition. Not always used. Temperature variable, up to about 15°C.

Early-weaned young are often kept in colony cages with approx. 14 rabbits/m² or on litter at 5-6 rabbits/m².

Other rabbits are kept in 40-50cm high, wooden or metal hutches, 0.75-0.93m² for doe and litter. Tight stocking prevents weight loss through play and exercise. Others kept in pens on shavings on wooden or earth floors, 0.14-0.25m²/doe.

Some farms breed earthworms in the manure pits under cages. Worms sold to fishermen etc. Worms also control fly problem in rabbitry.

Surgical

Toe nails clipped: can cause bleeding. Ears tattooed, or tagged with aluminium tags (can get torn off) or leg-rings applied (can cause pain and swelling) for identification. Tooth trimming. Castration of bucks in larger carcase production.

Feeding

About 70% of total costs. Pelleted complete foods (sometimes supplemented with hay), fed *ad lib f*rom about 2 weeks. Pellet hoppers and water nipples fixed to front of cages.

Average ration content: 60-70% cereal — barley meal, ground oats, maize meal, weatings, bran; 10-20% grass meal; 20% high protein feed — fish meal, soya bean meal; minerals and vitamins supplement. Medication — coccidiostat, antibiotics.

Breeding stock. Approx. 100-140g pellets/day. Stud bucks' and breeding does' diets adjusted to requirements to control weight. Pregnant does *ad lib*, consuming up to approx. 225g/day in last week. Lactating doe up to 450g/day. FCR 3.5-4.0.

Water. Adult rabbit drinks about 0.30 litre/day. Pregnant doe about 0.5-0.75 litre/day. Lactating doe about 2-5 litres/day.

Diseases, Problems

Mucoid enteritis. Respiratory problems. Hock sores. Abscesses. Ear canker. Coccidiosis (intestinal and hepatic). Typhlitis. Chronic rhinitis (snuffles). Mastitis. Venereal disease. Enteritis. Nephritis. Abortion. Fur-chewing. Fighting.

Slaughter

Approx. 5m/year. Sold and transported often long distances to specialist packers for slaughter. Age 8-10 weeks at approx. 1.8-2.5kg. May lose as much as 0.1kg *en route*, crated in 10s to slaughter and packing, going 8-10 hours without food and water. Large units do own slaughtering.

Breeding stock slaughtered at approx. 18 months-3 years old: commercial whites approx. 4.5-5kg: Californian 3.5-4.5kg. (Natural lifespan approx. 9 years, average weight of adult in wild 1.5kg). Output 5,000t/year.

Fur

Low value of rabbit skins due to young age at which slaughtered. Probably no rabbit farms in UK with fur as primary product. Hairs often used for felt. Older rabbits' pelts made into 'fun fur' coats, coat collars, gloves.

Wool

Angora rabbits selectively bred (English, German, Danish breeds). Small-scale UK. Rabbits caged individually. Wool clipped or plucked every 3-4 months between ages of 9 months and 4 years.

Rabbits are also bred for supply to vivisection laboratories (see **VIVISECTION** chapter).

2.8

FARMED ANIMALS: SHEEP

Descendent from the Asiatic mouflon. 1990 UK population 43.8m, including: 16.7 ewes; 3.6m shearlings; 22m lambs under 1 year; 0.49m rams for service; 1.4m others. 85,000 farms.

General
There are more breeding ewes in the UK than in any other country bar Australia and NZ, and more breeds of sheep in UK than any other livestock due to the variation in often poor conditions. Usually kept in the open air all year and fed mainly on grass, sheep are probably the least intensively farmed of all livestock.

Lambs are the most important and profitable produce of British sheep. Wool produces only about 3-10% of total receipts/year/ewe. (More in hill flocks). But wool is possibly the most valuable farm product of all.

The national flock includes about 50 pure breeds and about 300 crossbreeds. There is much crossbreeding and use of high quality rams on hardy ewes. The general cross-breeding programme, known as stratification, relies on ewes being drafted to lower grasslands for further breeding to produce fat lamb for slaughter. Lambs produced from hill and mountain flocks are brought down to easier conditions for growth and fattening. Constant movement of sheep from higher to lower land.

Breeds
• Mountain and moorland breeds. Slow growing. Long coarse wool. Lambing April. Typical breeds: Scottish blackface; Welsh. Ewe lambs retained. Draft ewes to uplands. Male lambs to lowlands. Herdwick sheep, unique to the Lake District, are the only breed able to survive on fells up to 610m where rainfall can average over 380cm/year. About 27,000 Herdwicks — one third of the total — are kept on 87 National Trust farms.[1]

• Grass hill breeds. Lambing is timed to meet growth of new grass. Cheviot, Clun, half-bred. Ewe lambs and ewes are retained or drafted to lowlands. Male lambs to lowlands.

• Down breeds (shortwools). Mainly for producing rams for crossing with other breeds for meat production. Quick growing wool. Suffolk, Oxford, Hampshire, Dorset breeds. Rams are crossed with ewes from uplands to produce slaughter lambs.

• Grass sheep on lowland farms. Lambing January-March. Intensive grassland system. 15-20 ewes/ha.

Breeding

Minimal use of AI. Rams (tups) used for breeding from 7-9 months. Pedigree and pure-bred rams are mostly produced from specialist farms.

Ewe lamb (female sheep in first year) is mated in first year (when still growing whilst producing a lamb) but more often first mated in second year. 1 ram lamb to 30 ewes; 1 ram to 40-60 ewes. The ewe comes on heat only late summer to winter — not all year round — for about 24 hours every 16-17 days until she is in lamb.

Rams are sometimes fitted with raddling harness-pad over chest with coloured grease to mark the ewes they serve. Rams and/or colour changed round after about 16 days. Rams tested for potential by semen collection via electro-ejaculation. Vasectomized rams often used to initiate oestrus activity in ewes.

Controlled breeding is practised on some farms, administering progesterone through vaginal sponge to control oestrus cycle. Hormonal manipulation of ovulation often used. Lambing induced by use of corticosteroid injection.

The ewe is in lamb for approx. 5 months. UK breeds lamb once a year (Dorset horn is an exception; can breed for 10 months out of the 12 and can lamb twice/year). Ewes are mated again 12 weeks after weaning lambs.

Ewes normally produce 1-2 lambs/year (twins in 45% of cases) according to breed and management. Sometimes 3 born together, seldom 4 or more. Lambs weigh 2.7-4.5kg at birth. Lambing January-May. Up to 4m lambs are lost/year — stillbirth, abortions, starvation, exposure, hypothermia, disease, accidents.

Ewe has 2 teats and can rear two lambs (sometimes triplets) but 'foster' ewes are often used. Foster mother might be tied in crate, unable to push foster lamb away. Will suckle her own and the foster lamb. Lactation 1.25-2.55 litres/day. Lamb takes ewe's milk in first 2-3 weeks of life with grass from about 10 days. Lambs may creep feed. Weaned at 4-16 weeks depending on system.

Under intensive systems, lambs are taken away from the ewes earlier and reared on milk substitutes and concentrates. In hill flocks, one lamb (of 2) is often weaned at 24 hours and fed on milk substitute and concentrates.

When lambing before grass is available, the ewe meets the energy demand by 'living off her back'.

General intensification trend by increased number of lambs reared by each ewe and by denser stocking rates.

15-25% of ewes are culled/year — lameness, udder troubles, poor yield, no lambs or poor quality ones — and replaced in flock.

Housing
Usually outside, but for intensive and/or in winter: yards, walled, platformed areas, pole barns, enclosed sheds; slatted or concrete floors; straw.

Each ewe approx. 1.0-2.3m² depending on size and state, with or without lambs. Pens of 30-50 ewes. Extra space for lambing pens. Lambs 0.5-1.0m²/lamb in groups of 6-15 up to weaning.

Surgical
Castration of male lambs, by knife; by bloodless (Burdizzo) method before one month old; or by rubber ring (Elastrator) in first week of life; by vet and anaesthetic after 3 months.

Tail-docking: shortening tail by rubber ring method, by hot iron or by cutting. Dagging: by shears. Ear punching, tagging, tattooing. Tooth-grinding prohibited in UK.

Feeding
Sheep feed largely on grass, with other bulky foods and small amounts of concentrates later in winter. Grazing is often enough until end of mild year. Through winter daily: 0.25-0.5kg hay; up to 4kg kale or silage; 0.5kg concentrates. Fattening sheep: daily equivalent of 0.5kg hay, 7kg roots, 0.25kg concentrates. For graz-

ing purposes, 1 cow = 5 sheep. Ram: high protein concentrates before and during mating season.

Flushing ewes. After lambs are weaned, ewes are put onto poorer grass during late summer to cut off milk supply and get them into lean breeding condition. 2-4 weeks before due to go to ram, fed well on, e.g. grass field prepared specially.

Steaming up. In-lamb ewes. First 3 months, grass feed only. Last 2 months, more feed needed; diet slowly improved during last 6 weeks with up to 1.5kg concentrate/day .

Lambs. Milk from birth from mother or artificial, then compound and increasing amounts of grass from 2-3 weeks old. Creep feeding of lambs, ends when lamb 16-18kg.

Water. Up to approx. 7 litres/day/ewe.

Diseases, Problems (* = notifiable)

Foot & mouth*. Anthrax*. Sheep scab*. Foot rot (commonest disease of sheep: treated by foot baths of copper sulphate or formalin solution; trimming overgrown feet with knife or clippers). Lamb dysentery. Pulp kidney disease. Navel ill. Scrapie. Twin lamb disease (pregnancy toxaemia). Tetanus. Mastitis. Blackleg. Lameness. Toxoplasmosis. Orf. Swayback (caused by shortage of copper in lambs). Pine (caused by shortage of cobalt). Hypomagnesaemia (shortage of magnesium). Hypocalcaemia (lambing sickness). Clostridial disease. Coccidiosis. Pneumonia. Hypothermia. E. coli. Broken mouth, teeth falling out at 6-8 years old; culled. Mites cause sheep scab. Ticks, keds, lice, maggotfly, blow-fly. Stomach and intestinal worms (sheep dosed with chemicals, e.g. phenothiazine). Liver fluke; 20% of sheep and 45% of cattle are affected in many areas.[2]

Wool

1990 wool clip: 54m kg (incl. 21m kg skin wool). Accounts for 5-10% of gross returns. 80% of growth takes place July-November.

Shearing. (Wild, natural sheep do not need to be sheared). May-July depending on locality, when yolk has risen in fleece, promoted by warm weather. (Winter shearing of housed ewes in SW England). First shearing in second summer of life at 14-15 months old, but some lambs are clipped in some breeds in south

England. Entire fleece removed in one piece. A contract shearer can average 100-150+ per day. Wool clip averages: longwool — 4.5-6kg; lowland grass sheep — 2.7-3.0kg; mountain sheep — 1.8-2.25kg. More from well-fed rams. Trials have taken place using French merino rams x north country Cheviots. Clip 4-10kg.

Approx. 27% of UK wool is skin wool (obtained from slaughtered sheep, mainly lambs and hoggets).

Dipping

Compulsory. Usually approx. 14 days after shearing, and in summer, to keep scab, maggot-fly, keds, ticks and lice under control. (Sheep are sometimes sprayed instead of dipped). Organophosphates used (as used in nerve gases and pesticides). Sheep cannot be sold at market within 2 weeks of dip. Once used, dip disposed of on farm land, often mixed with slurry. (See **Diseases**).

Milk

Specialized breeds: Friesland and British milksheep. About 200 farms, 50-150 sheep/farm. Yield/ewe up to 450 litres in a 180-220 day lactation. Dual purpose breeds; Clun and mule — 150-400 litres. Milk mostly used for cheese and yoghurt.

Usually in-wintered in groups on straw. Fed mostly silage and concentrates. Mated 3 times in 24 months.

Lambs in milking herd are weaned as soon as they've taken colostrum. Alternatively, weaned at 12-16 weeks. Or weaned at 5-6 weeks. Or ewes and lambs separated for increasing periods from 3-4 months of age (lamb). Most are fattened indoors for meat and killed at about 4 months. Ewes are milked mainly by machine twice/day leading to once/day during a lactation.

Slaughter

1990 figure: 20m. Lambs are slaughtered at liveweight 15-31kg. Barley lamb up to 35-40kg. Butchers lamb (suckling lamb) slaughtered after 2.5-4 months. Lambs weaned, stored and fattened, traditionally known as mutton but now still called lamb or sometimes at approx. 1 year, prime mutton. Ewes after 4-8 years. (Can live up to 15 years). Judas, decoy animals often used to herd sheep into lorry. 1990 output: 0.39m tonnes lamb and mutton.

Suede

In the UK, over 2m sheep and lamb skins/year are used for sueded garments. Shearling is the skin of a lamb or sheep that's been shorn once; lambskin is an unshorn skin. To make suede, the flesh side of the skin is rubbed to a nap.

FARMED ANIMALS: SLAUGHTER

(For statistics see slaughter sections under relevant species).

Slaughterhouse (abattoir)

Approx. 4,000 animals die every minute of every working day in slaughterhouses in the UK.

Slaughtermen receive no formal training; no qualifications are necessary. All slaughtermen have to be over 18, have worked, under supervision, in a slaughterhouse for at least 3 months, and be licensed as fit and proper persons by the local authority. Most work on piece-rates.

New hygiene rules in slaughterhouses as from 1991/2/3, enforced by the EC single market legislation. Every animal to be inspected by abattoirs before slaughter.

Until now, 9 out of 10 British abattoirs have escaped this antemortem requirement because they have no licence to export to the EC and must sell all their meat to British customers. The single market legislation will force nearly 900 domestic-only abattoirs to achieve by 1992 all the hygiene standards already required of the nearly 100 abattoirs which at present have export licences.

Nearly half of all abattoirs in the UK failed inspection by MAFF vets in 1989. About 300 of the worst slaughterhouses will be forced to close by 1992 due to cost.

EC rules would also require the government to stop subsidizing the cost of inspecting meat and checking for drug residues in carcasses.[1] Only 10% of UK slaughterhouses meet rigorous new EC standards.

Only 98 slaughterhouses are licensed to export to the EC. Nine have recently had their operations suspended temporarily after visits by EC health inspectors. Two were in Scotland.[2]

Over the last decade the number of animals slaughtered in the UK has increased by 25%; the number of slaughterhouses has declined from approx. 1,450 to just over 850.[3] Slaughterhouse premises 1980: 1,135. 1991: 778. After 1992 there could be just 300 left.[4]

1.7m tonnes of unwanted UK slaughterhouse material (including over 100,000t of blood) are generated/year.

All animals whose meat is to be sold for human consumption must by law (but see **On-farm slaughter** below) pass through a slaughterhouse, and all meat to be sold for human consumption must have been inspected and declared fit by a local authority meat inspector.

Animals are usually taken over short or long distances to slaughterhouses in lorries, direct from farms or from livestock markets. (Fewer slaughterhouses mean longer journeys). Unloaded into lairage where they stay until moved for slaughter. Poultry are usually left in transport crates until taken out and shackled ready for slaughter.

Animals are stunned unconscious, in different ways depending upon species, prior to death by throat-slitting (sticking; bleeding out; exsanguination). The time between stunning and sticking should be minimal. Ineffective stunning, especially by electric head-tongs method, means some animals are stuck after regaining consciousness. The period of unconsciousness following electric stunning is unlikely to be more than 20 seconds. The time between stunning and sticking has been found to be 30-60 seconds in some cases. Meat might be tenderized by electrical stimulation before animal is stuck, or by papain injection 20 mins before slaughter.

Stunning

• *Captive bolt pistol.* Two types; one is trigger-fired, and one fires when barrel is tapped on animal's head. A sharp hollow-ended steel bolt, propelled by a blank cartridge or compressed air, penetrates animal's forehead (cattle, pigs) or top of head (sheep, goats) — and automatically retracts — rendering animal unconscious, insensible to pain. A botched shot means slaughterman making further attempt(s).

• *Electrical.* Electric current is passed through animal's brain to produce unconsciousness. 3 types of equipment:

Scissor-like tongs, placed on both sides of animal's head. Low voltage tongs 75-90v must be applied for 7 seconds (in practice usually 2-4 seconds — demands of piece-rate practice of slaughterhouses) to achieve effective stun. High voltage tongs 250-350v should be held on for 2-3 seconds;

Head to body applicators 250-350v used with restrainer. Current flows through head to either back or leg, inducing stun and cardiac arrest;

Fully automatic systems, 600-900v, consist of motorized restrainer-conveyor with shaped electrodes hanging down inside tunnel which contact animal's head and back as it passes through.

Cattle

All adult cattle must be restrained in stunning box — a solid-sided metal pen with vertical sliding door at one end to allow animal entrance. Slaughterman stands on platform to one side and stuns animal with captive bolt pistol. Side of pen then opened to allow unconscious animal to be ejected into slaughterhall. Shackled by one hind leg, hoisted onto overhead conveyor, moved to bleeding area. Animal stuck — main blood vessels in throat cut — so that it dies from loss of blood. Cattle kill rates, approx. 70/hour. Approx 6% of cattle are not properly stunned prior to sticking.

Sheep

Carried to stunning area in V-shaped restrainer-conveyor or moved in groups to a pen where individually stunned by captive bolt pistol, or by electricity (tongs applied to temples). Then shackled, hoisted and stuck.

Pigs

Brought to stunning point by restrainer-conveyor or stunned individually in group pens by electricity. (In England & Wales pigs may be stunned using carbon dioxide gas; not widely used). Unconscious animals then shackled, hoisted and stuck.

Poultry

Hung by feet on moving shackle-line for up to 3 minutes (turkeys up to 6 minutes), heads carried through electric water bath for stunning. Throats then cut by mechanical or manual means. Some birds miss stun and/or the neck is cut inadequately. Birds then to scalding tank (boiling water to loosen feathers), some still alive and conscious. Approx. 30% of spent battery hens suffer broken bones before reaching stunner bath — due to rough handling. Up to 95% may suffer such injury before reaching the knife.

For details of slaughter of day-old males see **FARMED ANIMALS: POULTRY** chapter.

Rabbits
Stunned by electricity, neck dislocation or blow to back of head, then bled out.

Deer
In field, shot by rifle or, as in slaughterhouse, stunned by captive bolt; bled out.

Religious (Ritual) Slaughter
Jewish and Muslim communities are allowed by law (the Slaughterhouses Act 1974) to slaughter food animals without stunning first. Animals are fully conscious when their throats are cut. About 2% of cattle, 4% of sheep and goats and 1% of poultry are slaughtered/year thus. Pigs are not killed by ritual slaughter; pork not acceptable on religious grounds.

Conducted in licensed slaughterhouses by authorized slaughtermen of the Jewish and Islamic faiths. A cattle casting pen of the Weinberg, Dyne or North British rotating type is used for religious slaughter. These rotate through 180° so that the animal is lying on its back with the underside of its neck exposed for cutting. (Prohibited as from 5.6.92 in favour of upright restraining pen). Sheep, goats, small calves are laid on their backs for throatcutting in metal slaughter cradle; poultry are held under the arm, head downwards for cutting.

Jewish Method — Shechita
Approx. 50-60,000 cattle and calves, 25-30,000 sheep and lambs, 2.0-2.5m poultry are killed by this method/year.

Controlled by Board of Shechita. Slaughtermen (shochetim) undergo special training and are subject to license and annual examination by the Rabbinical Commission.

Animals must be alive, healthy and have suffered no injury at the time of shechita and no blood must be eaten. Meat declared fit for the food of Jews is called kosher. Unfit meat is called trefah. Meat discarded as trefah may be offered for sale on open market. Jews may not eat meat from hind quarters unless meat is porged. This procedure ceased in UK in1930s. Hind quarters discarded by Jews may also be passed for general sale. Effectively, 4 shechita-killed animals give same amount of meat (kosher) as one killed in usual manner would provide.

Act of shechita must be by a single rapid cut to the neck, severing both carotid artery and jugular vein with razor-sharp, blemish-free knife.

Muslim Method — Halal
Approx. 35-40,000 cattle and calves, 1.0-2.0m sheep, 8.5-9.5m poultry are killed by this method/year. Not controlled by central board but overseen by local Islamic community.

At time of slaughter, God's (Allah's) name must be invoked and the blood thoroughly drained from carcase afterwards. Meat thus obtained is called halal and the whole carcase is normally used. The act of halal slaughter is performed by rapid cuts at the throat severing carotid artery and jugular vein.

Cattle can take anything from 25-90 seconds, sheep and goats 8-10 seconds, and calves much longer, to lose consciousness after cut by religious methods. (Up to 6 minutes according to RSPCA).

On-farm slaughter
Some animals are killed on-farm for home consumption; some meat going to consumers and retailers. (Only by licensed persons in N. Ireland). Others are killed for humane reasons. Slaughter performed by farmer, knackerman, slaughterman or vet.

Red meat species are killed by captive bolt and bleeding out or by free bullet. Poultry by neck dislocation or by stunning by blow to back of neck, and throat cutting. Rabbits by neck dislocation or by stunning by blow to back of head or by electric tongs then throat cutting.

		No.
West Brom	Bourn'm'th	30
Wigan A	Bradford C	31
Barnet	Rotherham	32
Blackpool	Burnley	33
Cardiff	Hereford	34
Carlisle	Rochdale	35
Crewe	Lincoln	36
Doncaster	Halifax	37
Gillingham	Walsall	38
Mansfield	Aldershot	39
Northr'pton	York	40
Scarboro	Chesterfield	41
Wrexham	Maidstone	42
Corby	Halesowen	43
Poole	Crawley	44
Buxton	Goole	45
Hayes	Staines	46
Dundee U	Airdrie	47
Dunf'mline	Falkirk	48
Hearts	Aberdeen	49
Motherwell	Celtic	50
Rangers	Hibernian	51
St Mirren	S. Johnst'ne	52
Hamilton	Ayr	53
Kilmarnock	Morton	54
Meadowb'k	Forfar	55
Montrose	Raith	56
Partick	Clydebank	57
Stirling A	Dundee	58

SCORE-DRAW (1-1, 2-2, ETC.)........3 PTS NO SCORE-DRAW (0-0)........2 PTS
AWAY WIN OR VOID........1½ PTS HOME WIN........1 PT
(TREBLE CHANCE ONLY.)

11 JANUARY 1992

Home	Away	No	A	B	C	D	E	F	G	H
Chelsea	Tottenham	1								
Coventry	QPR	2	X							
Crystal P	Man City	3	X							
Liverpool	Luton	4	X							
Norwich	Oldham	5	X							
Nott'm F	Notts C	6	X							
South'pton	Sheff Utd	7	X							
West Ham	Wimbledon	8	X							
Blackburn	Bristol C	9								
Brighton	Barnsley	10									
Bristol R	Tranmere	11									
Grimsby	Oxford Utd	12									
Middlesbro	Ipswich	13	X							
Plymouth	Leicester	14	X							
Port Vale	Portsmouth	15	X	X						
Southend	Derby	16	X	X						
Sunderland	Millwall	17		X						
Swindon	Camb'ge U	18									
Watford	Newcastle	19									
Birmingham	Leyton O	20	X							
Brentford	Stoke	21									
Bury	Swansea	22		X						
Darlington	Torquay	23									
Exeter	Bolton	24									
Hartlepool	Chester	25									
Hull	Stockport	26									

Rodica pictured with 'Bergerac' actor John Nettles

3.1

FISHERIES: SEA FISHERIES

(See also **COUNTRY SPORTS: Angling** and **FISH FARMING**).

Annual worldwide catch of all fish is around 60-80m tonnes. Also, deliberate or incidental annual deaths of hundreds of thousands of seals, dolphins (500,000), porpoises and birds. In 1991, the 200-mile zone around Ireland was declared a whale and dolphin sanctuary. (And see **LAWS**, 1934). Many deaths are attributable to drift nets of up to 40km long. A UN resolution bans any extension of drift net operations pending a worldwide ban on their use to be introduced in 1992.[1] Diving birds such as razorbills, guillemots, puffins are snagged and drowned in static nylon gill nets used in UK waters. 2 main types of fish are caught.

Demersal Fish
Haddock, cod, whiting, sole, plaice and other flat fish live and feed on or near the sea bed. Nets used: trawls and seines. Shoals located by fish finder (electronic signal sent down to bounce off sea bed).

Pelagic Fish
Mackerel and herring live and feed closer to the surface, mainly in coastal waters. Nets used: purse seines and mid-water trawls. Shoals are located by sonar (movable sound beam).

A variety of other methods are used, e.g. static or drifting long-linesset at random depths and hooked with live or dead bait (generally catches larger fish); bottom drift netting with up to 200m long nets; anchored netting. Fish location equipment can show colours on monitor screen to denote species and sizes of fish. One catch could land over 200t of fish but this is increasingly unlikely.

The fish stocks found in the waters around Scotland are among the most heavily fished in the world. Cod and haddock should live for 10-20 years, reproducing every year from the age of 3 or 4. Fewer than 33.3% survive beyond 12 months, with a 60% chance of being caught in any year once reaching the 35cm size at which cod can be legally caught. A one year old haddock has only a 1% chance of becoming a four year old haddock.[2] Plaice could live up to over 20 years; skate 30-40.

Spawning stocks (estimated number of mature fish able to breed): cod — down to approx. 82,000t (lowest ever); haddock 117,000t. Since the mid '70s the number of young haddock entering the seas around Britain has fallen from approx. 122b to 7b.

Sizes and Quotas

In 1990 British fishermen were allowed to catch 36,300t North Sea haddock compared with 128,000t three years ago.[3] 1991 quota: 37,115t. The Scottish fishing industry is reckoned to need a total catch of around 100,000t haddock/year to be viable.[4] 1990 North Sea cod quota: 46,180t. 1991: 43,570t. North Sea Whiting 1991 quota: 34,010t; plaice: 32,720t.

Minimum landing sizes (N. Sea and West of Scotland) in cms: Demersel — bass 36; brill 30; cod 35; conger eel 58; dabs 15 (23 in N. Sea); flounder 25; haddock 30; hake 30; megrim 25; plaice 25; pollack 30; saithe 35; lemon sole 25; Dover sole 24; turbot 30; whiting 27; blue whiting 20; witches 28. Pelagic — herring 20; mackerel 30 (N. Sea only).

The UK fishing fleet consists of about 7,500-8,000 boats (thought by the industry to be 20-30% too large, and 40% by the EC) and most practice mixed fishing (fish for more than one species; e.g. fishing for cod and plaice Jan-April and for haddock March-June. That is, fishing is intensified when fish are pregnant. Landing fish full of roe makes fishing more viable).

The UK catches about 40% of its fish in the North Sea (largest fishing port is Peterhead, Scotland). Most others are caught in the Irish Sea, West of Scotland and English Channel. Highest % of boats (33.3%) are trawlers, which have become more powerful, dragging larger nets. The traditional diamond shaped mesh of the trawls does not allow young fish to escape to breed. Up to 60% of a catch — unsaleable small fish — might be dumped overboard.

Each vessel whose overall length is over 10 metres and whose cod and haddock landings from areas IV (North Sea) and VI (W. Scotland and Rockall) over the period 1.1.89 to 30.6.90 exceed (i) 100 tonnes and (ii) 40% by weight of their total landings... [will remain] in port for at least 8 consecutive days per calendar month during the period 1 February to 31 December 1991.[5]

An option to this 8 day tie-up has been the use of 110mm mesh nets. From 1.7.91, a regulation 90mm square mesh panel is to be used in all nets of 90 and 100mm diamond mesh in specified North Sea and West of Scotland areas (with a possible derogation for 80mm square mesh panel in nets of vessels heavily dependent on whiting). Other net size regulations apply to nephrop fishing and to Irish Sea.

1989 Catch (1990 figures not available).
Figures shown here for wet fish and shellfish are rounded up; MAFF and SOAFD figures not entirely agreeing.

UK sea fish landings by UK vessels: total 581,000t. (Scotland 465,600t; England & Wales 99,700t; N. Ireland 15,600t). Of which:
• Demersal: 313,500t — mostly haddock (72,030t) and cod (68,250t) but also whiting (38,510t), plaice (26,180t), anglers/monks (12,820t), saithe (11,770t), sandeels (24,560t) and others.
• Pelagic: 267,400t—mostly mackerel (158,030t), herring (99,340t) and others.

Foreign vessels landed 45,800t at UK ports.

Death

Nets close around fish which are sucked out by pump into the boat, or net lifted up or hauled aboard by winches and power blocks to land fish on boat. Air pressure leads to swim-bladder expansion, and bleeding from the gills. Fish die of shock, asphyxiation and/or crushing by weight of volume of catch landed onto boat. Others killed by ice bedding. But many are still alive when landed and gutted e.g. cod, haddock, plaice, skate, sole. Others die slowly, caught up in gill-netting left several hours. Fish usually 1-5 years old. Monkfish chopped in half, heads discarded. Eels killed by partially burying in salt (about 2 hours) or chopped up into pieces and boiled.

Salmon & Trout

Caught by coastal netting at rivers, estuaries around Scotland. 1988: total sea trout approx. 49,000 (54t). Total of salmon and grilse (fish which have spent only one winter at sea) approx. 165,000 (525t). UK catch of salmon by same methods plus angling, approx. 1360t (England & Wales: 367t; Scotland: 882t,;N. I.: 114t).[6] Scotland: salmon caught by rod or net 280,000 in 1989; 145,000 in 1990. Drop thought to be due to drift net trolling a 200 mile sweep from the Humber estuary to Holy Island preventing salmon getting back up river to spawn. Such monofilament netting is illegal in Scotland.[7] 1990 UK salmon net catch approx. 950t.[8]

Shellfish

UK shellfish landings1989: 92,000t. (Scotland 45,000t; England & Wales 40,700t; N. Ireland 6,300t).

Mostly Norway lobster (27,020t) but also crabs (14,600t), cockles (14,800t), lobster (1,400t), scallop (8,600) and others (38,000t). Foreign vessels landed 1,100t at UK ports. (1990 figures probably not available until 1992).

Shellfish minimum landing sizes (in mm) — Norway lobster 25 carapace (N. Sea), 20 (W. of Scotland); lobster 85 carapace; scallop 100; velvet crab 65; brown crab 125-165 (regional differences).

Crabs (4-5 years old) caught and taken from baited underwater trap-pots or creels. Usually kept alive (often with claws nicked) in tanks or boxed on wet shavings or straw, and killed for cooking by drowning in fresh water (3-5 hours) or by spiking nerve centre of brain with pointed rod.

Cockles raked or dredged from sandbanks at about 4-5 years old. High-pressure steam-killed.

Lobster caught in pots or creels at 5+ years old. Packed and despatched cool and damp. Killed and cooked by boiling alive.

Scallops. Dredged. (And see **FISH FARMING**).

Norway lobster. Caught in pots, light trawl or netted with other fish. Head and shell twisted off. Low survival rate of those discarded due to small size.

Shrimps. Trawled at low tide. Killed/cooked in boiling water.

Whelks. Caught in baited pots, 1-10 years old; boiled in seawater.

3.2

FISHERIES: FISH FARMING

Over 3,000 years old in China. Started in 19th century in Europe after development of artificial fertilization. About 90 species of fish are farmed worldwide. 2 main types of UK fish farming:

Total culture. Fish in lifelong captivity. Sold for food or broodstock;

Partial culture. Fish in part-of-life captivity, released to return later as marketable fish or to replace wild stocks (about 60 farms rear coarse fish in England; 100-400t UK) or to stock 'catch your own' farms.

There are 1,000-1,500 fish farms around or in UK (5-600 in England; 5-600 Scotland; 50-60 Wales; 30-35 N. Ireland), producing approx. 70,000t fish/year. Main fish farmed are salmonids — salmon and trout. Other fish farmed: carp (100t+); marine fin fish (100-1000t); eels (60t+), and shellfish (see next chapter). Little planning control of marine-based farms.

SALMON

Atlantic salmon (*Salmo salar*) are used in salmon farming. In the wild, they return to fresh water during the 12 months before spawning in October-December (or into February). The female (hen) deposits eggs in river gravel. Growth stages: egg—alevin—fry—parr—smolt—grilse—spawner—kelt.

Young fish hatch and remain in gravel, feeding off their yolks, emerging as fry and feeding on insect larvae. Mortality approx. 90%. The freshwater, or parr, stage lasts 1-4 years before migration to sea as juveniles (smolts: majority in Scotland aged about 2) in May-June. Might return to native rivers as grilse after first 6 months at sea, weighing about 1.5-7kg, or as older fish — salmon — after up to 5 years at about 25kg. Females, most weighing 3-6kg at maturity, produce about 1,500 eggs/kg body weight. When spawning is complete, fish known as kelts.

Commercial salmon farming was pioneered in Norway. In the UK, there are approx. 350-450 coastal salmon farms, mainly around N. and W. Scottish coast and islands, including approx. 200 sites in Scotland producing 22m smolts/year and 60 sites in England and Wales producing 2m smolts/year. Shetland produces about one fifth of total (but biggest fish).

1991-2 UK production potential is 42-54,000t (1990: about 40,000t; 1989: 29,000t). But actual production likely to fall to about 33,000t in 1991 and 29,000t in 1992. Value of annual Highlands and Islands output has now overtaken the value of the region's total output of beef and lamb. Leading companies: Unilever (Marine Harvest); Booker McConnell, and Norsk Hydro.

Breeding and Stocking

Approx. 100-200m ova/year are stripped (squeezed) from breeding females under anaesthetic. Most are rejected, some are exported, and about 35-55m are laid down for hatching. Mixed, fertilized with milt stripped from males and incubated. The resulting ova are then developed in landbased, freshwater hatcheries. Production rate is managed by water flow, temperature and light.

Alternatively, genetically female fish are induced at fry stage by a diet dosed with sex steroid to produce 'female' sperm to fertilize female eggs which grow to be females. Some spawning is induced by hormone injection and most by artificial daylight.

Reared in 4-10m diameter, (fresh)waterflow tanks, e.g 5-20,000 fry/tank (15-30kg/m³), with about 20m/year sold as approx. 12-18 month old smolts in May-June and transported by lorry, wellboat or helicopter after 24-48 hour starving and mild anaesthetization to sea, loch or river-estuary cages in a floating raft system. Other transport of live fish in small tanks in cars, pick-ups, vans, large tanks on lorries, or in custom-made tankers.

Grown on for 14-20 months. Cages approx. 200-2000 m³ cubic or cylindrical net bags, open at top, suspended from floating collar with shape maintained by ropes and weights. High mortality, 20-50%, due to overcrowding and transfer to sea water.

Alternatively, fish in land-based units kept in tanks into which sea water is pumped. Land based units especially use daylight manipulation to encourage breeding at artificial times.

Attempts are being made to prevent salmon reaching maturity — farmed salmon start to lose quality at the grilse stage — yet maximise growth by, e.g. a period of feeding only during alternate weeks, and/or hormonal sterilization. Many fish which do not develop into smolts at end of first year are released into wild.

Fish and cages are cleaned with chlorine, sodium hydroxide, iodine solution, calcium oxide.

Feeding and Production
Feed = about 40% of costs. Fry are fed little and often, up to 6 times/hour, by automatic feeder (also hand feeding). Smolts are fed 5-6 times/day (10kg/week/1,000 smolts), then once in sea cages fed 2-4 times/day on sandeel, fishmeal (whitefish by-products, sprat, pout, capelin, herring, mackerel), fish oil, feathermeal, other animal wastes and soya bean meal in pelleted form (up to 6kg/day/1,000 fish) plus a dye additive — canthaxanthin (E160g/161g) — to colour the flesh pink, compensating for lack of colour in farmed fish — recently banned by the Scottish Salmon Growers Association; astaxanthin pigment used instead. Plus antibiotics, e.g. oxytetracycline, and vitamins, minerals. Leading fish feed manufacturer is BP.

6t salmon might be produced from a 200 m³ cage stocked with 4-8000 smolts. A typical farm might carry 100t at a time and can produce up to 400t (some up to 800t) /year with 250,000 salmon contained in 30-100 sea cages, eating 10-15t of food/week.

Production of approx. 40,000t salmon requires at least 56,000t feed (55% being fishmeal). FCR 1.5-5.0.

Diseases, Troubles (* = notifiable)
Lice can cause up to 50% mortalities. Farmed salmon are treated for sea lice with the chemical preparation Aquaguard (or Nuvan), a pesticide containing the organophosphate toxin, dichlorvos — lethal to shellfish. A withdrawal period of at least 4 days should elapse between dosing the fish and harvesting. Salmon are bathed in the dichlorvos solution approx. every fourth week in summer and every third month in winter (rarely necessary on land-based farms). Solution remaining after treatment is released into the sea.

A new development is to introduce the live-caught or specially-bred wrasse fish into the cages to swim amongst salmon. The wrasse eats sea lice which cling to the salmon's body. Approx. 1 wrasse is needed for every 50-80 salmon. Possible threat to wild wrasse population. (In the wild, the salmon shakes off lice when swimming upstream). Vaccines also being developed.

Furunculosis* (bacterial disease affecting up to15%. Vaccine being developed to avoid use of antibiotics). Bacterial kidney disease (BKD)*. Whirling disease*. Enteric redmouth (ERM)*. Infectious pancreatic necrosis (IPN)*. Malnutrition. Blue sac disease. Fin rot. Cannibalism. Vibrosis. Starvation. Gill tissue damage from high nitrate and ammonia levels in water (result of overstocking). Skin ulceration, kidney infection, tumours. Stress. Tail and fin nipping. Cannibalism. Water quality and temperature. Diseases controlled with formalin, malachite green, antibiotics (often injected). Handling at loading-unloading is a main cause of damage.

Seals (300-5,000/year), otters (Scottish sea lochs once supported Europe's best otter populations), mink and diving birds are killed — shot, trapped, poisoned — in an attempt to protect farmed fish stocks. Also, wild salmon and sea trout are often prevented from returning to rivers to spawn by anti-predator nets round cages of farmed stock. Farmed fish escapees and hatchery effluent can cause genetic contamination of wild salmon, depressing natural numbers.

Production of 1t of farmed fish can mean the concentrated discharge of 0.75t of solid waste (faeces, unconsumed food) into the sea.

Slaughter

Slaughter of fish is not controlled by specific regulations.

Salmon are harvested at 1-4 years at grilse stage (and later) when stocking densities are at about 6 or more salmon/m³. Average 26-32 months old at 2-5kg. Fish are starved for 24 hours-1 week prior to slaughter.

Stunned by blow to head with blunt instrument (priest), by asphyxiation, or by placement in tank with CO_2 bubbling through water, or by electric current, then bled to death by cut to gill arch or to aorta. Or bled to death without stunning. (And see **Trout**).

TROUT

Commercial trout farming was pioneered by Denmark. In the UK, mainly rainbow trout (*Salmo gairdneri*) are farmed; non-native fish introduced in the 19th century from N. America for stocking angling waters.

In the wild, spring-spawning. Females produce 2,000-12,000 eggs usually only once, hatching over 4-7 weeks. Males are mature from 1 year; females from up to 6 years. Reach up to 20kg. Some leave fresh for sea water coasts and return to spawn after up to 1 year at around 200g. Others,around 3-15kg, travel 000s of km.

There are approx. 250-400 mainly land-based, chalk-stream freshwater farms in S. & E. England and C. & S. Scotland producing about 16,000t /year.[1] (1980 figure: 4,400t). About 23 inland farms in N.Ireland produce approx. 1,000t/year. Others, producing larger fish, use sea cages off west coasts of Scotland and Wales.

Female fish mainly. An average 10-15t production unit requires some 18m litres/day of pure, aerated water.

Breeding/Stocking

Brood fish or ova (about 28m/year) are supplied by specialist egg hatcheries — many from USA, Denmark and Taiwan. Mostly female. Broodstock stocked at 8-10kg/m^3.

At spawning in winter (usually hormone- and lighting-manipulated) ova are squeezed (stripped) from body after 3+ days starvation. Fish sometimes anaesthetized. Male milt is added to ova at 1 male to 3 females rate. Fish back to tank, pond, raceway or cage for recovery and preparation for next breeding.

Genetic manipulation and hormone feed allow production of only female fish. Breeding females are sex-reversed to produce 'female' milt to fertilize female eggs to give all female output. In sex-reversed fish, masculinized females are killed by blow to head, cut open and testes removed for mixing milt with eggs (or stored). Average female brood fish produces 2-3,000 eggs.

Healthy ova take about 3 weeks to develop 'eye'. Then shocked by dropping into water to kill weak and infertile eggs. Good eggs are transferred to farm rearing units, hatching within 2 weeks into tiny fry. Fry feed for 3 weeks on internal yolk sacs then develop into 'fingerling' stage when solid feeding (automatic or manual), light and temperature manipulation and water flow begin. Stocked at approx. 25kg/m³. (Up to about 60,000/70m³). Water flow in tanks, ponds, races, forces fish to swim to build up flesh.

From fingerling to 285g trout takes 10-15 months. Mortality about 30%.

Feeding and Production

Fry are fed up to 10 times/day; fingerlings 6-8 times; growers 3-5 times and brood stock 1-2 times/day. Solid feeding begins with 55% fishmeal+fish oil+plant protein diet, plus vitamins, as powder then pellets. (Also wet fish diets). 0.4kg-9kg feed/100kg fish/day depending on age and water temperature (4°-18°C), over a 12-month period. Some trout feed includes carotenoid supplement to reproduce the pink pigmentation of wild trout (achieved by feeding on shrimp). FCR 1.5-3.0.

Diseases

Gill disease. Fungal growth, controlled by malachite green. Gut damage treated with oxytetracyclene (and see **Salmon**). Tail and fin nipping. Cannibalism.

Slaughter

Starved for 3-6 days before killing at 8-15 months at 180-400g.

Fish graded, killed (blow to head with priest; exsanguination with or without stunning in CO_2-saturated water; electrocution). Or removed from water, packed and iced on farm, and transported to market — Billingsgate, Manchester, Glasgow — taking up to 14 minutes to die, often in transit.[2] Fish also sold live to processors to kill, clean and pack for supermarkets.

Other farms provide facilities for 'catch your own' trout, where rod and line are hired by the hour. (And see **COUNTRY SPORTS: Angling**). Production also of larger 1-2.7kg trout.

Trout farmers kill prey species — as for salmon above, except seals — plus eels, perch, pike by trapping and electro-fishing.

FISHERIES: SHELLFISH FARMING

Mainly crayfish and molluscs. 470-550 mollusc (marine) farm sites — 200-250 around England; 250-350 Scotland; 10-20 Wales; 5-10 N. Ireland — and 60-70 crayfish (freshwater) farms in UK. Shellfish farming generally exploits naturally available food in the water and requires less or no medication. 681t shellfish were grown in Scotland in 1989. 1990: around 1,000t. 1991:1,396t.

Diving duck and other shellfish predators die by drowning in submerged anti-predator nets

CRAYFISH
Mostly in south England, farms produce mainly the non-native signal crayfish (from USA and Australia) for the table (rather than solely for on-growing; some mixed. Approx. 40,500 crayfish produced for on-growing). Table production is 4-7t/year. Each fish at approx. 70-100g at 1-3 years.

Breeding. Mate in autumn (1 male to up to 5 females). About 50-300 eggs/female, laid 4-5 days later. Females put into mesh cages for when eggs hatch late spring. Juveniles moult after 6-8 days, cling to female until moult 2, then leave mother (who's released back into ponds) and moult several times again, then 2-3 times/year until mature. Stocked in water-flow or static ponds, gravel pits 1.5-5m deep or canal channels 1.5-2m deep x 3-10m wide x 50-150m long, up to approx. 5,000/ha of water surface.

Feeding. On natural sources — crustaceans, vegetable matter, with little supplementation (potato, carrot, trout pellets).

Diseases, Troubles. Crayfish plague. Signal crayfish are carriers, and escapees can contaminate native stocks. Porcelain disease. Cannibalism. Exoskeletal disease.

Caught in trap-pots. Sold live. Boxed up, sent to restaurants etc. Killed by boiling.

NB. Soft-shell crayfish research development in USA forces

moulting rates by hormone feed, injection, water bath, and abla-
tion — removal of moult-inhibiting eye-stalks.

LOBSTER

Tonnes of lobster kept in recycled seawater in tray storage systems. Take about 5 years to grow to saleable size. Many supplied
live to restaurants, hotels. Production 1986: nil. 1991: 1m (same for
crabs).[3] Experiments taking place into lobster ranching on sea
bed.

MOLLUSCS

Feed by filtering particulate matter from seawater. Prone to
bacterial and viral contamination where sewage is discharged
into coastal and estuary waters. Some are heat-treated, relaid in
clearer water or purified for human consumption.

Oysters

Cultivated since Roman times.

Approx. 100 farms in UK. UK Pacific oyster production estimated to reach over 30m (at about 95g each) by 1993. Pacific oyster
(non-native) based on cultivation from seed stock from warm-
water hatcheries. Natural oysters based on on-growing of juve-
nile stock taken from wild.

Oyster farming: natural oysters about 120t/year; Pacific oysters about 500-1,000t/year (Scotland: 1.3m [107t] in 1989; 1.41m
[113t] in 1990. About 45% coming from one producer). Also Black-
water estuary, and Devon.

Oyster larvae and seed bought in from e.g. USA. 2-4 years from
start to harvest. Oysters feed themselves, suspended in nets and
trays from raft or in trays set on trestles or stacks on sea bed.
Stocked at about 15t/ha.

Most of what is eaten of oyster (live) are the gonads.

Mussels

Long-line, raft and bottom-culture (mud) systems.

100+ farms, output 1,100-5,000t/year (Scotland 440t in 1989;
457t in 1990). About 30-50t/ha. Seed mussels bought in at 10-
20mm.

Mud. Mussels naturally root to sea bed by byssus or beard. At low tide, exposed to air, they clam up. When covered, open up to siphon water through body at 1 pint/15 minutes, filtering out food particles but also taking in any toxins. When harvested at about 2-3 years old, purified in salt water for 36 hours.

Raft. Large-scale type 50t, 20 x 27m raft might grow up to 100t mussels, with 800 growing ropes and 200 seed-collector ropes suspended to 15m depth. Mussels reach market size at 18-24 months. Sold live and cooked-killed by steaming.

Scallops

Total UK production about 10t/year. (Scotland production 1989: 57,200 [6.9t]. 1990: 105,500 [12.7t]). On-growing natural stock in lantern nets at about 100/m² in final year (or laid out on sea-bed) at about 2-5 years old. Growing process can involve being drilled for 'ear-hanging': hooked through drilled hole to hang on string or nylon lines. Killed by shell being prised open by knife, boiling or steaming, and viscera removed.

Queens

Total UK production about 170t/year. (Scotland production 1989: 2.37m [94.8t]. 1990: 1.36m [54.4t]). On-growing natural stock.

Clams

About 4 farms in England produce 100t+/year, from hatchery-produced seed. Manila clams; about 2 farms in England produce 0.16t/year, from hatchery-produced seed. Around 10-25t/ha.

Shellfish 'pests': American tingle, Crepidula, Mytilicola. Diseases: Bonamia. paralytic shellfish poisoning.
(And see **SEA FISHERIES** chapter).

4.

FUR FARMING

In September 1990, the European Parliament voted on an Environment Committee Report to ban from January 1995 the import of fur (see **EXPORT-IMPORT** chapter) from 14 species of animal — badger, beaver, bobcat, coyote, ermine, fisher, lynx, marten, muskrat, otter, raccoon, sable, squirrel, wolf — usually caught in leg-hold traps. (Endorsed by Council of Ministers — except France — in June '91. Next meeting, October). May be amended.

Britain outlawed the leg-hold trap over 30 years ago but it is still used extensively in the USA, USSR, Canada and 7 of the EC countries, trapping 20-40m animals/year. Bans exist in approx. 65 countries. Trap is not instant-kill. Animals may die of exhaustion, thirst, starvation, hypothermia, attack. If alive when trap is checked, animal is killed by beating or crushing. Animal may bite off own limb in bid to escape. The EC Report called for funds for Canada to investigate 'humane' traps. At present, several variations of the steel-jawed leg-hold trap are used abroad:
• leg-hold trap in drowning set — animal trapped to fall into water where drowned or asphyxiated;
• jump trap and stop-loss trap—designed to catch animal further up leg;
• pole trap — set on tree or pole, animal trapped and falls to dangle;
• spring pole trap — attached to bent sapling which springs up to hoist and hang trapped animal by leg.

In all cases the animal may be trapped by other parts of body than the leg, as with the Conibear trap — designed to instant- kill by springing shut to break neck or back. Many non-target ('trash') animals are caught by mistake. It is still legal in UK to manufacture and export such traps. Up to about 100m animals/year are killed for fur worldwide, trapping and farming.

Numbers of animals used to make one fur coat: baby ocelot 12; mink 65; fox 10; karakul-Persian lamb 30; raccoon 40; lynx 15; possum 25; cheetah 6-12; leopard 3-5.

Some species — coypu, mink and muskrat — imported into UK for fur farming, have been released or have escaped into wild, forming established colonies. Mink are still found throughout the UK; an eradication campaign was abandoned as hopeless in 1970 (see **COUNTRY SPORTS: Hunting**); muskrat were eradicated by trapping by 1939; coypu presumed eradicated by trapping by 1989 (campaign killed over 31,000). Rabbits, introduced for meat production and used also for fur production, established wild populations in the 11-12th centuries, now widespread throughout UK (see **COUNTRY SPORTS: Shooting**).

100,000 or more British and Irish red foxes/year claimed to be snared, or trapped illegally with gin-traps for the fur trade.

MINK

American mink. Farm-raised mink have been bred to be larger than mink in wild. Mink breeding started at turn of century in Canada; 1920s in UK. Non-domesticated animals kept in cage environments: barren; restrictive space allowance and exercise facilities. Behavioural abnormalities, including self-mutilation, are common. (See **COUNTRY SPORTS: Animals** for details of mink in the wild).

35-40m wild animals/year — mostly fox and mink — are bred and farmed for fur worldwide. Denmark is the main area of European production (about 10m mink).

There are 31 licensed mink farms in the UK, (mostly in Yorkshire and Lancashire; 8 in Scotland; 1 in N.Ireland). Approx. 100,000 animals, producing about 0.15m skins/year. UK mink farms are licensed under the Destructive Imported Animals Act 1932 and Mink (Keeping) Order 1987.

Breeding

Season March-April. Most breeding in UK between 5-10 March. Males taken to females. 1 male to 5 females. Often mated again a week later to ensure success. Gestation lasts 36-76 days (delayed ovulation and implantation). One litter/year. 4-6 in litter.

Kits are usually born in May, weighing 10-15g (doubled in 4 days). Suckling 6-8 weeks. Start solid feeding at about 3 weeks (when birth weight multiplied by 10 or so). Weaning at about 6-7 weeks. Separated from mother around July to be kept, usually, in pairs. Growth period ends September followed by fur production stage: Sept-November. Mortality about 9-12%.

Artificial selection is directed towards coat colour, fur quality, fecundity and disease resistance. Gives rise to mutants, illnesses, deformities.

Housing

Rows of 25cm-wire mesh cages, usually 2 animals/cage (or mother and litter) with wooden, wire-based nestbox attached or inside. Straw or hay bedding may be provided at whelping and winter.

Mink cages measure approx. 46-76 x 23-46 x 30-46cm (about $0.05m^3$ minimum). Each mink is 34-75cm long.

Housed beneath open, roofed shed. Breeding animals kept singly in cages.

Feeding

Generally, except when breeding, mink are fed to excess to produce larger animals; more fur. It takes 650kg-1t of feed to produce a full length mink fur coat.

Slaughterhouse wastes, day-old chicks and other poultry by-products, bonemeal, cereals, fish, animal fats, molasses, beet pulp, horsemeat.

Consumption about 10%+ of body weight/day.

Diseases, Troubles

Distress. Repetitive stereotypic behaviour. Self-mutilation. Ear chewing, fur clipping, tail sucking, biting. Fighting. Deafness (hedlund white mink). Foot and other deformities. Dropsy. Scrotal hernia. Freakism. Constricted glands. Cannibalism. Wet belly disease. Liver haematomas. Aujeszky's disease. Viral enteritis. Plasmacystis. Pneumonia. Tuberculosis.

Slaughter

(Natural longevity 11 years). Killed at 7 months in November after winter moult. Barbiturate (pentobarbitone sodium) injection; carbon monoxide inhalation (car exhaust) in box, and neck dislocation methods. No bleeding out. Pelted whilst warm.

FOX

2 fox farms in UK. (No licensing). Fox cages measure approx. 114 x 106 x 71cm. In wild, fox ranges over 800-6,000ha territory.(Natural longevity 14 years). Killed during their first winter. Electrodes to mouth (clamp or rod) and anus (rod), connected to portable 12v (car) battery via step-up transformer producing about 200v. No bleeding out. Pelted whilst still warm.Annual production 2-10,000/year. (Further information on UK fox farming not available).

The current fur farm licensing system comes up for review in1993.

5.

ANIMALS PERFORMING

CIRCUSES

Originated in Rome's Circus Maximus, 329 BC. Today's familiar format took shape in 18th century with juggling, acrobatics, and equestrian events. The first performing, exotic animals appeared in the early 19th century along with the birth of the travelling circus in the USA. Menageries linked up some decades later.

To some extent the circus trade is international, with UK circuses having travelled abroad, a few foreign circuses performing here (especially the Moscow State Circus) and animals traded between circuses. Some space is given below to details of non-UK circuses and not all the information applies to purely UK-based ones. Circus overseas tours — though infrequent — can involve thousands of kilometres travelling.

The Soviet Union has about 70 permanent circuses and 32 travelling ones, using 7,000 animals belonging to 140 species. Over 300 animal-circuses operate in Italy, over 100 in Germany, 7 in Switzerland, over 250 in India (India banned circuses from training or exhibiting certain animals, including tigers, bears, monkeys, panthers, dogs in April 1991; similar bans have existed in parts of Scandinavia for years).

There are approx. 16-20 animal-act circuses in the UK, 12 of which are members of the Association of Circus Proprietors whose guidelines prohibit menageries of non-performing animals. Approx. 2-300 animals are kept in UK circuses — elephants, big cats, bears, alligators, crocodiles, snakes, horses, ponies, llamas, pigeons, camels, dogs, pygmy hippo.

Circuses were left out of the Zoo Licensing Act 1981. The Act covers only zoo animals and does not extend to the caging and stabling facilities of identical animals in circuses. Animal trainers are not required to specify or to show how animals are trained. No law governs circus animal accommodation and travelling conditions. There have been two convictions for cruelty.

Under the Performing Animals (Regulation) Act 1925, trainers must be licensed, and police or local authority officers can inspect circus animals at all 'reasonable times' whether the site is council- or privately-owned but are not allowed on or behind stage during public performances. ACP state that member circuses are available for inspection by the RSPCA at any time. RSPCA claims that officers do not have similar statutory right of entry but may observe training, yet are invited only to daily rehearsal rather than to initial training. The Act contains no stipulations for size of enclosures or the number of hours an animal can work.

ACP considers that new legislation concerning the training and keeping of performing animals is required. It is quite easy for anyone to set themselves up in business as a circus proprietor. Some have done so merely by having a few trained animals. Some show a complete disregard for standards.[1]

Approx. 150 local councils in UK have banned wild animal acts from their land (some still allow performing domestic animals).

Animals

Animals are taken from the wild (see **EXPORT-IMPORT** chapter), or bought from zoos and safari parks or other circuses or, as with most UK circus animals (except for some African elephants), bred in captivity. Some circus animals are on endangered species list. Many die during capture and/or in transit. Family groups are broken up. Animals often castrated. When animals surplus to requirements, they have been or are sold to animal dealers, to zoos, to vivisection labs, to travelling menageries, to exotic restaurants, or killed (pelts might be used for fashion clothing), or retired to circus 'farms' (largely the case with UK circuses).

Training

Animals are submitted to two phases; taming and training. Both can involve deprivation of food and company; use of intimidation, drugs, muzzles, coaxing, rewarding, punishing, shackling; physical force with the use of apparatus including whips, electric goads, hooks, sticks, pulleys, pedestals, gun noise.

By baiting and luring, the triggering of escape and aggression impulses, or by direct physical force, the animal is made to perform the required movements repeatedly until eventually all that is required is the appropriate 'trigger'.[2] Fire extinguishers and beating sticks have been used on out of control tigers.

In the Ring

Animals are often forced and/or frightened into ring, to perform acts natural and unnatural to them, under simulated conditions, for human entertainment and, as far as the ACP is concerned, education.

Horses made to walk backwards on hind legs with heads tethered to maintain curve of neck; elephants made to balance on tubs or walk with front legs on back of another elephant; chimps (none in UK circuses) made to ride monocycles; bears made to ice-skate or dance or ride scooters; kangaroos made to box; one species made to ride on the back of another; others made to walk tightropes.

Animals spend a total of about 30 minutes/day in the ring, in about 2 performances.

Out of the Ring

Animals travel over short and long distances in confined spaces in beast wagons — lorry trailers open (barred) one side only, the other 3 being blank wooden or metal walls.

From the ACP code: lions, tigers, leopards and bears — sleeping quarters, and access to exercise area of 6.1 x 12.2m or 12.2m diameter, with toys, furniture etc. Beast wagons minimum of 2.4m wide x 3.05m long/animal or 2.1m long/animal where 2 or more are kept together. Shelves should be provided for leopards. Sizes not specified for other animals.

Other recorded accommodation: bears kept individually in 1.3 x 1.0 x 0.75m cages. Most bears live in the beast wagons, restrained by chain collars and leads during performance and between wagon and ring. Some animals, e.g. elephants, are shackled to stakes 60% of the time. 7 polar bears in 6 x 2.5 x 1.8m wagon; 14 lions in 9 x 2.75 x 1.5m wagon; 0.34-0.9m³ for 2 tigers. Animals kept in wagons in street in readiness for rehearsals at, e.g. the Palladium (horses, camel and baby elephant, Royal Variety Show 1988). 4 tigers found stranded in 1989 for 16 hours in a trailer in a Scottish lay-by. 5 poodles kept in a 1.5 x 1.2m cage. Alligators and crocodiles, mouths taped up, kept in small tanks. Added stresses of frequent noise, movement and lights. In circus season, animals might spend about 20 hours/day in beast wagons.

Extensive travelling within and outwith home country, as far afield as the Far East, S. Africa, Australia, by ship in confined conditions. Examples; 4 lion cubs in 2.4 x 1.3m container; 3 elephants spending 3 months in metal container wagon measuring 12 x 2.4 x 2.7m high, on a 40,000km world trip; 17 tigers abandoned in 2 trailers, 1 tiger being eaten by the others.

Out of season, winter housing largely unrecorded but restrictive. Animals normally spend 2-3 months stationary in winter quarters, often confined and/or shackled in available buildings, cages, lorries. May leave winter quarters for short Christmas season.

The Blackpool Tower circus gave its last performance at the Tower on 3-4 November 1990 after 94 years because its Tower lease was not renewed following protests from animal rights groups. Performing animals were kept for 5 months of the season in cellar beneath the ring without fresh air or sunlight. Also a non-performing pygmy hippo was kept solitary in an underground 6 x 4m enclosure. The circus intends to move to the Pleasure Beach.

DOLPHINARIA

Started around 1962 in UK. Operated under local authority permit — Zoo Licensing Act 1981.

Dolphins, whales. Taken from wild (seas around Mexico, Guatemala, Taiwan, Japan, Thailand, Caribbean etc.) with high wastage, early mortality, wounds, injuries. Family groups broken up. Schools chased by power boats; netted or roped and transported in crates on stretchers to zoos, circuses, dolphinaria. Often drugged, treated with vitamins, antibiotics etc.

2 dolphinaria exist in the UK (30 in the early 1970s). Chemical-laden waters. Dolphins and killer whales have been kept solitary

(often as punishment) without contact with their own kind. Training might include the use of hunger and forced feeding.

Officially, up to 300 dolphins and 8 killer (orca) whales have been imported into the UK since 1962. Only 11 have survived captivity, training and performance. No import permits for dolphins or killer whales have been issued since 1983 and none will be unless new minimum standards (see below) are met.

Dolphins live for up to about 12 years in captivity, usually much less; natural life expectancy is 25 years. Killer whales live for up to about 6-8 years in captivity; natural life expectancy is 50-80 years.

Shows invariably include loud music, animals wearing outsize sunglasses; jumping through hoops; teeth-brushing etc.

New standards by 1993. Minimum pool size requirements — larger than those currently in use, e.g. 22 x 9 x 3m deep for 3-4 dolphins; 26 x 14 x 3.5m deep for 8 mixed cetaceans — for enclosures containing up to 5 dolphins (average body length taken to be 3.5m): surface area equivalent to 7m diameter circle, average depth 5.6m — volume of 1,000m³.

Requirements for killer whales (average body length 7.5m): surface area 15m, depth 12m — volume 12,000m³.

Problems, Troubles

Deformities. Injuries. Disturbed, stereotypic behaviour identified in circus animals due to lack of natural surroundings, lack of space and destruction of social structure. Licking cage bars; running at cage bars; head swinging, shaking; paw sucking; begging noises; weaving movements; whirling; pacing. Aggression. Apathy. Boredom. Infant neglect. Travelling accidents. Shackle sores. Herpes. Liver failure, kidney deficiencies. Deaths.

Cetaceans: skin disease and other problems associated with synthetic sea water. Aggression. Stereotypic behaviour. Suicides. Trauma. Bullying. Heart attacks. Noise pollution (music and filtration system). Ingestion of foreign objects thrown by crowds. Boredom. Susceptibility to human diseases. Miscarriages, stillbirths, infant deaths.

As is usually the case these days, there were no animal-act circuses shown on Christmas TV in 1990. Channel 4 showed the French-Canadian Cirque de Soleil which has rejected the use of animals on moral grounds.

Other non-animal circuses include: Circus Archaos, Centre National des Arts du Cirque (both French), The Shenyange Acrobatic Troupe (Chinese), Circus Benneweis (Danish), Os Paxaros (Spanish), Ra Ra Zoo, Circus Senso, Ship of Fools, Circus Burlesque, Zippo's Family Circus (all British), Hot & Neon (American-Canadian), Circus Oz, Flying Fruit Fly Circus (both Australian).

ANIMALS ON SCREEN

Cruelty to animals in films and/or in their making falls under the Cinematograph Films (Animals) Act 1937 and the Video Recordings Act 1984 (and Protection of Animals Act 1911). Some main concerns here are the tripping of horses; training methods; conditions whilst not performing (relevant also to use of animals in advertisements). Many films are made — because less costly — in other countries, where no such legislation applies. Films are vetted in the UK by Classification (Censor) Board and RSPCA. Animals used thus may be, or later become, circus animals here or abroad.

6.

PETS

On 5 December 1990 *Which?* magazine published a nationwide survey of 100 pet shops which showed a general squalor, over-crowding of animals and poor advice. The Pet Animals Act 1951-1983 requires animals to be kept in 'suitable' conditions but does not define them. There are approx. 3,390 pet shops in the UK.

Pet Populations[1]

1989

51% of all (about 21m) UK households kept at least one pet.

Approx. 7.4 m dogs   (in 6m households)
      6.9 m cats   (in 4.6m households)
      1.9 m budgerigars (in 1.3m households)

1990

52% of all (about 21.5m) UK households kept at least one pet.

Approx. 7.4m dogs   (in 5.9m households*)
      6.8m cats   (in 4.6m households**)
      1.7m budgerigars (in 1.1m households)

(Incl. approx. 400,000 cats and dogs in N. Ireland).

* 80% have 1 dog; 20% have 2 or more.

** 33% have more than 1 cat.

Fish (figures not available) are the third most popular pets.

The most popular breeds of dog in the UK are: German Shepherds, Labradors, Yorkshire terriers, spaniels, Jack Russells.[1] Rabbits are kept in approx. 0.95m households; hampsters in 0.44m, and guinea pigs in 0.23m.[2]

Outlandish pets and other exotic animals held privately have to be licensed under the Dangerous Wild Animals Act 1976-84. Nearly 1,000 such animals were registered in Britain early in 1989, including squirrel monkeys, wolves, racoons, lions, leopards, bears, elephants, yak, tapir, prairie dogs (at least 8 of which have gone missing in the last 2 decades).[3] About 300 people keep llamas as pets.[4] (And see **Appendix D: UK EXOTICS**).

10,237 diurnal birds of prey are kept by approx. 4,000 people in Britain (registered under Wildlife and Countryside Act 1981). About 400 are reckoned to be falconers — people who fly raptors to take live game. (And see **COUNTRY SPORTS: Falconry**).

Dog Breeding

A Kennel Club survey[5] in 1987 (covering 362 breed clubs; 114 breeds) identified cause for concern in respect of a number of bitches being used too soon after previous litter, and/or before mature. Survey identified an element of indiscriminate breeding in a third of litters. Dog breed groups analysed: hound, gun, terrier, utility, working, toy.

Bitches too young when bred, highest in gundog group: 10.2%.

Bitches too old when bred, highest in gundog group: 4.6%.

Litters consecutively bred, highest in toy dog group: 16.1% (relates to total sample of 11,400 litters).

Bitches having too many litters, highest in toy group: 6.7%.

Bitches having excessively large litters, highest in gun dog group: 7.4%.

Mutilation of Pedigree Dogs

Most common mutilation in UK is the docking of tails. Ear cropping is now rare, mainly on dogs being exported to countries where this is a requirement. Both procedures are only carried out on certain breeds. Docking is a requirement of the breed society regulations. Normally performed on young puppies without anaesthesia. Neither procedure of benefit to the dog; alter balance and reduce ability to communicate. Illegal ear cropping inexpertly practised by those involved in dog-fighting.

Puppy Farms

Establishments where litters of puppies are bred and/or sold to dealers and not to the final owners. Also, 'puppy supermarkets' (dealers and others offering several different breeds for sale, 'many other breeds available' etc.). Over-breeding. Dog breeders are licensed under the Breeding of Dogs Act 1973 (registered with local councils) but many running puppy farms are not. Dogs sent unaccompanied by road, rail, air for breeding and / or sale. Bitches sent out on loan.

Pedigree bitches (may also be Kennel Club registered) kept to produce as many litters as possible, often physiologically exhausted. Kept for life in restrictive housing — caravans, sheds, cages, tea chests etc. Poor diets. Mated twice / year. When too old or fail to produce, are dumped or killed.

Puppies removed too young — at about 5-6 weeks — and sold in poor condition to dealers who have bought from other puppy farmers. An estimated 100,000 puppies / year are involved. (Problems include skin diseases, parasites, heart defects, food intolerance, gastric problems, eye defects, hip dysplasia, campylobacter, parvovirus, twisted intestines).

Pups transported long distances, left overnight crated in vans, kept in crowded conditions. Dealers re-sell to kennels, pet shops or puppy 'supermarkets' or send abroad, possibly for experimentation. Many puppy farms are situated in Wales (approx. 400 licensed breeders in West Wales and about 3 times this number of unlicensed premises). Puppies sold for several hundred pounds.

Stray Dogs

Due to early puberty, large litter size and short pregnancies, dogs multiply 15 times, and cats 30-40 times, faster than humans.

Over a 7 year period, one unspayed female dog could produce the following offspring: under non-controlled conditions, approx. 4,400; under controlled conditions, approx. 72. Available methods of controlling birth rate have been: (a) to decrease birth rate; (b) to increase death rate. The UK has relied mainly on the latter.[6]

There are approx. 500,000 stray dogs in the streets and countryside of the UK. 80,000 people are bitten each year, 10,000 livestock killed or maimed and 350,000 road accidents caused by dogs of irresponsible owners.[7] The RSPCA estimates that approx. 1,000 dogs are needlessly destroyed each day by vets, animal welfare associations, the police and local authorities.[8]

In 1990 the RSPCA (Supported by the National Farmers Union, the Police Federation and the British Veterinary Association among others. Opposed by, among others, the British Field Sports Society) pressed unsuccessfully for the establishment of a dog registration scheme in Britain(the only dog registration scheme in the UK operates in Ulster), using the following statistical case.

Summary of Costs[8]
Present approximate costs of strays (dogs registered with police only).

Keeping, destroying or re-homing 240,000 dogs	£ 6 m
Dog warden service	£ 6 m
Road accidents caused by dogs	£50 m
Hospital treatment of other injuries	£ 7 m
Injuries to livestock	£ 1 m
Total costs about	£70 m

Costs of dog registration system and dog warden service

Total annual cost of registration system (with tattoo)	£11 m
Total annual cost of maintaining registration and warden service	£31 m
Total costs about	£42 m

In May 1991, the government announced an immediate ban on the import of pit bull terriers and Japanese tosas and a potential ban on owning fighting breeds, and the elimination of the breeds from the UK by neutering orders. (And see **LAWS, Dangerous Dogs Bill 1991**).

Problems
Fish, many imported, kept in water tanks, bowls or ponds. Goldfish are still given as prizes by travelling shows, fayres. Pets kept captive in cages, hutches, kennels, on chains, on balconies. Many neglected, abused, unexercised. (See **Appendix A: ILLEGAL CRUELTY**).

Horses, ponies, donkeys, mules kept often without shelter, food, water or veterinary attention. Problems are accentuated by tethering — restricted movement, unable to seek more hospitable conditions. Cross-bred animals are not bred for hardiness. Tether tangles round obstructions. Injuries to feet and mouth due to grazing on waste land. Ingestion of chemicals when grazing grass verges. No marking. Law enforcement difficult.[9]

Horses feet problems. Laminitis or 'founder'. Most common cause is excessive feeding of already fat, children's horses.

Other animals, especially dogs, are bred with deliberate defects and features detrimental to their health.

There are an estimated 1-2 million feral cats in the UK.[9]

Feeding

Total consumption of prepared dog and cat foods 1990 [1]
(000 tonnes)

Canned ('moist') dog food	533
Semi-moist dog food	5
Complete dry dog food	132
Mixers for dogs	126
Canned ('moist') cat food	51
Other cat foods	30
Dog treats	46
Cat treats	1

Cat treats are based on milk, meat, biscuit and cereal. Dog treats are based on chocolate, meat, biscuit and cereal.

Pet industry estimated consumption of raw materials — cat and dog foods: (000 tonnes/year)[1]

Meat and meat by-products	472
Fish	66.8
Cereals	174

Pre-packaged bird seeds sold in 1988/89: 2,541t; 1989/90: 2,401t. Includes seeds for domestic caged birds and wild birds and millet sprays representing approx. 15-20% of total market for bird seeds.

The Pet Food Manufacturers Association has 67 member companies which account for 98% of the national pet food market. The PFMA *Profile* 1990 states that

"Member companies use only materials from animals which have been inspected and passed as fit for human consumption...This rules out the use of any materials from horses, ponies, whales, seals, kangaroos, cats, dogs and many other species...the industry uses only materials of beef, lamb, poultry and pork origin, fish and others such as rabbit. The materials used are those parts of the carcase which are either surplus to human requirements or which are not normally consumed by humans in the UK. Examples are lung, liver, heart, intestines, carcase trimmings, blood".

Materials come from UK, USA, Canada, New Zealand, Australia and various European countries.

Table 8. Pets: Humane Destructions[1]

by RSPCA (England & Wales)

1989: Dogs 52,844; Cats 35,539; Others 18,839.
* Figures include: 36,235 dogs and cats too sick or injured to live; 12,114 unwanted new-born puppies and kittens; unwanted pet animals for whom no homes could be found; all species, not simply pet animals.

1990: Dogs 40,879; Cats 32,769; Others 18,816.
* Figures include 29,610 dogs and cats too sick or injured to live; 11,105 unwanted new-born puppies and kittens; unwanted pet animals for whom no homes could be found; all species, not simply pet animals.

by Ulster SPCA (N. Ireland)

1.1.89 - 31.3.90
Dogs 16,510 (includes 3,577 at owners' request).
Cats   8,814 (includes 1,773 at owners' request).
1990-91 figures not available at time of writing.

by Scottish SPCA

1989: 3,935.
1990: 3,953.

by Aberdeen SPCA

1989: Dogs 41; Cats 179.
1990: Dogs 44; Cats 144.

7.

VIVISECTION

General Information

The practice of experimenting upon live animals dates back at least to AD 130-200. Over 100m animals/year are now used worldwide; approx. 3.3m/year in UK, where 60-70% of procedures are conducted without anaesthetic. There are approx. 20,000 persons licensed to perform animal experiments, and around 370 vivisection laboratories in Britain; 16 in N. Ireland. (And see Tables at end of chapter).

Vivisection here relates to experimental or other scientific procedures which 'may have the effect of causing pain, suffering, distress or lasting harm' performed on 'any living vertebrate other than man' and includes foetal, larval and embryonic forms from the halfway point in gestation or incubation period re mammals, birds, reptiles; and when capable of independent feeding re fish and amphibians.

No area of animal experimentation is banned by British law, except the use of animals purely to gain or demonstrate manual skills; but allowed for such in microsurgery. (Non-vertebrates are experimented upon without the same control, e.g. eye experiments on octopus).

Only approx. 20% of procedures conducted are required by legislation, i.e. Medicines Act 1968; Health & Safety at Work Act 1974; Agriculture (Poisonous Substances) Act 1952; Food Act 1984 and their overseas equivalents, and assorted others. There are no legal requirements for the remaining 80% or so; e.g. biomedical research, and toxicity testing of cosmetics, toiletries, household products.

A largely secretive industry. Kinds and amounts of research conducted by individual laboratories are not divulged by government. In 1981, the Home Office ended its practice of issuing a list of laboratories where animal experiments are conducted. No admittance to laboratories is afforded to the RSPCA or public; only to Inspectors (see below). Many experiments are not published.

Controlling Legislation

The Animals (Scientific Procedures) Act 1986, which replaced, on 1.1.87, the Cruelty to Animals Act 1876. An Animal Procedures Committee (APC) has the power to investigate and report on such matters as it may determine, as well as upon those requested by the Secretary of State. The APC must consist of a Chairman and at least 12 other members, one of whom must be a lawyer. No more than half the members should be licensees, or have held a licence in the past six years; at least two-thirds of its membership must be medical practitioners, veterinary surgeons or biologists. Animal welfare interests are represented.

Documents relating to the Act are a *Code of Practice for the Housing and Care of Animals Used in Scientific Procedures* (1989) which, amongst other things, suggests provision of exercise areas, furniture, bedding etc. and *Guidance on the Operation of the Animals (Scientific Procedures) Act 1986* (1990).

Experiments and other scientific procedures on living animals are conducted by holders of a licence of personal competence issued by the Home Office, for research which has also been granted a project licence, under which applicants (little or no independent scrutiny of project licence; Inspectors approve applications, and certain categories of experiment — tobacco, cosmetic testing, microsurgery — are referred to APC at application stage) predict which of 3 categories of severity — mild, moderate, substantial — the procedures are expected to fall within, and only conducted on registered (certificate of designation) premises. Animal breeders and suppliers are also registered.

Experiments are funded by government departments, medical charities and industry and conducted at universities and polytechnics (most experimenters work and/or are trained in academic institutions where approx. 25% of all animals are used) and commercial, contract laboratories (where about 60% of all animals are used). The Medical Research Council has 30 research centres. Some companies and charities have their own labs.

Home Office Inspectors (19 in Britain and 3 part-time in N. Ireland) visit the premises. Some Inspectors (who hold medical, biological or veterinary qualifications) specialize in a particular area, e.g. cosmetics testing or behavioural research.

Fourteen cases of infringement of the Act or licence conditions were dealt with in 1989. In one case the person's licence was revoked. Admonishments were given in the other 13 cases and in a number of cases additional conditions were imposed on the relevant licences to ensure that any recurrence was unlikely. In 1990, at least 2 licences were revoked (for experiments wherein the abdomens of insufficiently anaesthetized rabbits were heated with an electric lamp.)[1] The 1990 *Statistics* give no information on such matters.

Since 1876, when the Cruelty to Animals Act was passed, over 170m animal experiments have been carried out in the UK alone. Of these, 85% have been performed since 1950.[2]

Animal Supply
Animals are specially bred (dogs and cats — with exceptions — must be), and sent by road, rail, air to labs by accredited breeders (about 33 in UK), for experimental work. But other animals are also imported (with high mortality) from the wild, breaking up social groups. Monkeys are trapped in nets or cages; larger, older ones are shot or poisoned; their young, e.g. infant chimps 2-3 years old, are taken and transported (e.g. 10 young baboons to a 1 x 0.6 x 0.5m crate for up to 48 hours), quarantined, then on to laboratory. Other animals are trapped in the wild in UK; others come from overseas breeders; others are known to have been stolen pets; others known to have been retired racing greyhounds; others from zoos; others bred on site.

Breeders also supply surgically prepared animals according to lab requirements: castrated; glands removed; bred specially to have reduced blood pressure; susceptibility to cancer etc.

On 13.4.88, the first patent (No. 4736866) for a living mammal was granted in the USA for a strain of mice genetically manipulated to develop cancer (Oncomouse; Harvard University). An EC proposal exists for similar European patenting.

UK breeders also supply labs overseas. In September 1989, 79 beagle puppies (paired in 0.9 x 0.6m cages) suffocated to death in transit to a Swedish drug company. The breeders involved here were subsequently given an accreditation certificate, but in May 1991 faced financial collapse, with the RSPCA stepping in to save and find homes for the 400 dogs left on the premises.

Animal Housing

Most animals, before and / or during procedures, are kept in barren, often tiered cages or plastic containers, often isolated. Rats and mice are kept in groups in low-ceiling, cramped cages; rabbits singly with just enough room to turn around or 3-6 in a 1 x 0.6 x 0.3m cage; 5 guinea pigs in 0.6 x 0.45m cage; dogs, 2 or more to 4.5m² floor space; primates rarely in social groups, many in isolation, solitary confinement. Little or no bedding, exercise. Artificial light; pelleted, semi-synthetic food, supplemented with minerals and vitamins. Such conditions can lead to self-mutilation and other abnormal psycho-behavioural patterns.

Other animals have been found trapped in cages — monkey in 0.9 x 0.76 x 0.76m cage. Others spend 3 months to life in 1m³ cages. (No monkey should be housed in a cage which has any dimension shorter than twice its crown-rump length.)[3] Other species, e.g. ferrets and cats, are often housed in groups. The housing *Code of Practice* (see above) offers the following cm² floor area range of guidelines/animal: monkeys — 1,350-14,000; mice — 60-200; rats — 100-800; rabbits — 1,300-6,000; cats — 3,300-7,500; dogs — 10,000-80,000; chickens — 250-2,800; and pigs — 1.0-7.5m²; horses — 12-20m². Temperatures range from 10-24°C for horses to 20-28°C for New World primates.

When not undergoing procedures licensed under the Act, animals in laboratories are subject to other standard legislation, e.g. Protection of Animals Act 1911.

Areas of Use

The main areas of research using animals include: developing new products; testing safety of new products and their ingredients; pure research undertaken with no specific aim in view apart from the attainment of knowledge, and applied research.

A vast range of experiments and procedures are conducted (see

Tables 9-12). Animals are burnt; scalded; poisoned; shot; inflicted with diseases like cancer, diabetes, syphilis, herpes, arthritis, influenza; have eyes removed; eyelids sewn up; nerves crushed, severed; bones broken; are subjected to stress; given electric shocks; drugged; brain-damaged; irradiated; have electrodes implanted in the brain; parts of brain removed; are traumatized; deprived of food, water, heat, maternal care and companionship in UK laboratories. (Surgery requires anaesthesia). Some experiment types are outlined below.

• *Draize eye irritancy test*. Introduced in 1944. Usually conducted on albino rabbits with large eyes which produce tears less effectively than humans' (so cannot wash substance away). Substance under test — including shampoos, pesticides, weedkillers, detergents, oils, riot control gases — is sprayed or distilled into one eye (other eye acting as the 'control' eye) of conscious rabbit, with irritancy effects and damage noted for up to 7 days. Usually no pain relief.

• *Draize patch test*. For skin irritancy. Hair clipped from area of body of animal (generally rabbits or guinea pigs) confined in stocks. Exposed skin is sometimes abraded. Substance is taped (e.g. on gauze) to skin and effects observed for signs of damage. Lasts up to 14 days. Usually no pain relief.

• *Toxicity tests*. Including the Lethal Dose 50% (LD50) and Lethal Concentration 50% (LC50) tests. Introduced in 1927. Not required by legislation. Force-feeding, skin application or forced inhalation of substances like pesticides, drugs, weedkillers, household and industrial products. Single dose. Oral method by inserting tube down throat. Rats and mice are often used as, unlike humans, they cannot vomit up the substance. Or by injection. LC50 conducted by forced breathing of vapour by batches of animals to note level of dose which kills 50% of them. Lasts up to 14 days. Test sometimes poisons animals through sheer quantity of substance rather than its specific toxic effect. LD50 is an acute toxicity test. Sub-acute tests last 1-3 months; chronic toxicity tests, e.g. for carcinogenicity, can last 3 months-life.

• *Efficacy tests*. Used to support specific claim for a product, e.g. anti-perspirant effects tested on mouse footpads (only area of mouse body with sweat glands); anti-plaque properties of dental products tested on mice or rats fed a high sugar diet; sun-cream applied to skin of mice wrapped in tin foil and taped down under sun-simulation machine.

• *Writhing Test*. Chemicals known to cause pain are injected into animals; new painkiller drug is injected to see if it stops animals writhing.

Drug Production

Main area of medical research (which takes up about 75% of all experiments on animals) and includes development and safety testing. Drug licensing regulations are controlled by the Medicines Act 1968. The Committee on Safety of Medicines (CSM) approves and monitors the safety of drugs but excludes consideration of whether new drugs are any better than existing ones. Up to 80% of new drugs on the market are new versions or combinations of existing ones. The CSM expects drug companies to prove the safety of drugs with details of extensive animal tests and clinical trials in humans before a licence is approved.

Over 18,000 licensed medicines are available in UK, using about 3,000 active components. All prescription and other orthodox drugs have been and are tested at some time on animals.

Thousands of compounds are tested each year to find new chemical entities (NCEs). Symptoms or diseases are artificially induced or implanted in animals (animal 'models') by surgery or by dietary, hormonal or chemical treatment, or by breeding (see **Animal Supply**). A new drug might be tested on 1,000 animals. Initial testing is mainly conducted on rats and mice to assess drug's potential to cure or alleviate.

Hundreds of compounds proceed to the next stage of toxicity testing, on guinea pigs, rabbits, cats, dogs, fish, birds, monkeys. Initial toxicity test, e.g. LD50, is short-term; a single dose in 2 species of animal. Other tests long-term: repeated dosing for side-effects; teratogenicity tests for deformities in offspring; tests to investigate effects on metabolism.

A small percentage of drugs will go on to clinical trials, in humans, with only approx. 5% becoming a prescription drug. The research programme for each drug may take 3-12 years. Up to 50% of all antibiotics produced are used for farm animals.

Secrecy among pharmaceutical companies results in almost no sharing of research data — therefore a duplication of tests. There is no established data bank on animal experiments and alternative testing methods.

Agrochemical Testing

Toxicity testing of some products is demanded by various Health & Safety legislation and the Agriculture (Poisonous Substances) Act 1952. The data requirements for approval under the Control of Pesticides Regulations 1986 list a wide range of animal experiment possibilities including the LD50.

At least 2 common lab species (e.g. rabbits, mice) are subjected to the LD50 — the pesticide administered orally or applied to the skin. LC50 test also used, forcing animals to inhale vapours, dusts, sprays for, e.g. 4 hours in exposure chamber, prevented from grooming by restraints.

Also, skin and eye irritancy tests; 90-day experiments — substance administered orally to two species (one of which being a non-rodent); tests for cancer (carcinogenicity tests); tests for birth defects (teratogenicity tests); organophosphorous compound pesticides which can damage the nervous system, tested on hens.

There are no safety data on about 44% of chemicals in pesticides, food additives, cosmetics and drugs. 80% of other commercial products lack any sort of safety information.

At least 4,000 people/year suffer acute poisoning from pesticides in the UK.[4] Long-term effects are unknown.

Livestock Research

Farm (and other) animals are used in laboratory experiments to seek new breeding techniques and levels of performance.

Experiments at the Institute of Animal Physiology at Babraham in Cambridgeshire, for instance, have involved pigs being fitted with brain electrodes, goat udder transplantation to the neck, and observation holes opened into the sides of cattle and sheep.

Other examples include drug testing to try to eliminate 'vices', e.g. tail-biting, of factory farmed animals; exposing newly-shorn lambs to below zero temperatures; removal from mother at birth. In 1990, 109,295 birds were used in Gumboro disease experiments (see **FARMED ANIMALS: Poultry** chapters; **Diseases**).

Wallabies from Whipsnade Zoo have been experimented upon at the Institute of Zoology in Regent's Park, London to investigate controlled cycles of reproduction. Also primates have been deprived of their sense of smell to increase breeding patterns (unsuccessful).[5] The Zoological Society of London has collaborated with companies in tests on rats; force-feeding chemicals used in plastics, dyes and explosives re effect on fertility.[6]

Research is now being conducted into transgenic animals (giving rise to 'new', patented animals) and gene reconstitution whereby an animal's product, e.g. milk, is 're-designed' to have different properties or to contain human proteins or to become a new product entirely.

Cosmetics

Cosmetics produced in the UK come under the Consumer Protection Act 1984 which means that they have to be safe. The manufacturer decides how to determine this and whether or not to use animals. See Draize, LD50, Efficacy tests, above.

Warfare & Space Research

Animals are shot, gassed, burned, infected and irradiated. Hundreds of research scientists have contracts with the Ministry of Defence. Most work of this type is conducted at the Chemical Defence Establishment at Porton Down (not bound by controlling legislation) in Wiltshire on monkeys, sheep, baboons, goats, pigs, rats, mice, guinea pigs, dogs and rabbits. Animals are wounded, killed by live ammunition, rubber bullets and ball-bearings. Anaesthetics are often used during shooting but some animals are allowed to recover consciousness for assessment of treatments and techniques. Others are exposed to nerve gases, forced to breathe chemicals used as military smokescreens. Others exposed to radiation and others used in germ and biological warfare research.

The USSR, USA and others have sent animals, including dogs and monkeys, into space. Animals are used for similar, land-based, research in UK (at for instance, the British Space Biomedical Institute in Sheffield), exposing them to simulated space environment effects. Space research also includes using live animals in crash conditions.

Alcohol Research

Generally, animals — rats, baboons, rhesus monkeys, dogs and others — are forced into consuming alcohol, often by injection or vapour inhalation. Research includes study of links between alcohol and aggression; cirrhosis of the liver; high blood pressure; alcohol effects upon the foetus; alcoholism (see below).

Behavioural Research/Experimental Psychology

Animals are used to determine, for instance, how starvation affects aggression. Animals are brain-damaged to study the effect on memory and behaviour. Electric shocks are used in punishment and conditioning experiments. Animals deprived of food, water, stimulus, mothers. Induced drug-addiction; withdrawal.

Other experiments include amputation, burning, scalding, organ transplants. (See Tables).

Effects

Recorded effects (apart from deaths) in animals include: lethargy, diarrhoea, severe respiratory distress, quivering, muscle contraction, anal haemorrhage, penile haemorrhage (skin LD50 with paraquat weedkiller); sores, hairs erect, tremors, convulsions (irritancy tests with Lindane insecticide); convulsions, tears, diarrhoea, discharge and bleeding from the mouth and eyes, crying out, paralysis (LD50); ulceration, haemorrhage, swelling, discharge from eye (Draize test). Insanity. Organ damage. In cancer research, tumours may ulcerate and occur in brain, tail, eye, muscle and grow to comprise 10% of body weight; such animals may lose up to 20% body weight.

Once experimented upon and if able or allowed to recover, animals may, with Home Office consent, be sold or given to others for further experiment (depending on type of original procedure; and then under terminal anaesthesia); or re-homed if suffering no adverse effects, or killed by anaesthetic overdose injection, gassing (CO_2), neck dislocation, blow to back of head, electrical stunning and bleeding out, or decapitation, depending on species. Animal carcases are usually disposed of on site by incineration, or by licensed animal by-product processors.

Dissection

Compulsory dissection has been removed from the syllabus of all A level exam boards. Not compulsory at GCSE level. Dissection continues, enforced by some teachers. Thousands of animals are bred and killed to be dissected in science classes. Supplied as preserved specimens, or freshly killed in schools.

Animals in schools are often kept in inappropriate housing/environment. Inexpert handling. Amateur stockmanship, especially at holidays and weekends.

Table 9. Experiments and Procedures on Living Animals in Great Britain[1]

Categories	1989	1990
Total numbers of procedures on animals (incl. experiments)	3,315,125	3,207,094
Number of procedures without anaesthetic	2,094,866	2,205,360
Total number of animals used*	X	3,100,553
Fundamental research	702,715	625,240
Applied research	2,612,410	2,414,008
Selection of medical, dental & vet products	1,158,561	1,079,235
Animals used in toxicity testing of medical products	289,716	291,032
Animals used in toxicity testing of non-medical products	254,482	266,843
Animals used in education & training	12,099	10,382
Procedures on cats	4,762	4,392
in respiratory & cardiovascular research	1,839	1,803
in nervous system & behavioural research	998	869
Procedures on primates	5,280	5,284
in toxicity tests of medical & vet products	1,949	2,123
in toxicity tests of non-medical products	226	28
in nervous & behavioural research	1,154	909
Procedures on dogs	12,625	11,433
in respiratory & cardiovascular research	3,800	3,697
in toxicity tests of medical & vet products	4,563	3,327
in digestive research	2,080	1,333
Procedures on mice	1,744,880	1,636,332
Alcohol research	1,114	1,429
Toxicity tests of cosmetics & toiletries	12,090	4,365
Toxicity tests of food additives	5,710	10,822
Toxicity tests of tobacco & its substitutes	387	659
Toxicity tests of household products	4,017	1,486
Deliberately causing animals to have cancer	73,531	59,616
Test for cancer-causing chemicals	47,285	37,478
Procedures deliberately causing psychological stress	8,325	11,093
Application of substances to the eye	107,015	115,991
of which, Draize tests on rabbits	4,273	4,008
Injection of germs into brain or spinal cord	55,150	64,586
LD50 and LC50 toxicity tests**	73,130	98,631
Procedures required by legislation, British & overseas	670,000	686,733
No. of project licence holders (in charge of research projects)	4,205	4,500
No. of visits to laboratories by inspectors	2,775	2,829
Reported infringements of the law or of licence conditions	14	X
No. reported to the Director of Public Prosecutions	0	X
No. of licences revoked	1	2+?

* Details re number of animals used available for first time in 1990 *Statistics*.
Some animals are used more than once, see p 123 and Table 11.
** 1989 and 1990 figures are not directly comparable. 1990 figures include all
quantitative short-term tests which have death as end point.

Table 10. Laboratories and Selected Procedures
Great Britain[2]

	1989	1990
Designated places*	375	381
Conducted by commercial laboratories	2,007,302	1,866,208
	(61% of total)	(58% of total)
Conducted by medical schools, universities,		
polytechnics	747,593	748,025
	(23% of total)	(24% of total)
Training stimuli (incl. electric shocks)		
involved in	30,723	18,533
Physical trauma/human injury simulation	1,817	910
Exposure to ionizing radiation	73,760	58,452
Thermal injury/burning/scalding	394	602
Virus for vaccine production grown in eyes		
of unanaesthesized birds	100,200	109,295
Genetic engineering/harmful genetic effect**	92,636	191,882

Other Toxicity Tests of various Products (in addition to those shown in Table 9)

	1989	1990
Drugs and medical appliances	289,716	291,032
Household products	4,017	1,486
Industrial chemicals	86,252	91,999
Agricultural substances	80,692	108,858

* Figures not directly comparable. 1990 figure includes breeders, suppliers and laboratories which also supply animals to others.

** Figures not directly comparable. 1990 figure includes transgenic animal procedure statistics for the first time.

Table 11. Main Species Used Great Britain[2]			
Species	**Number of Procedures**		**No of Animals**
	1989	**1990**	**1990**
Amphibians/Reptiles	11,545	13,123	9,304
Birds	251,954	247,609	242,145
Cattle	5,019	5,177	4,985
Cats	4,762	4,392	3,456
Dogs	12,625	11,433	8,567
Ferrets	3,520	3,263	3,048
Fish	77,525	107,989	107,345
Gerbils	5,619	5,630	4,734
Guinea pigs	144,827	137,704	130,425
Hamsters	20,255	17,722	17,185
Horses, donkeys and crossbreeds	1,411	1,169	826
Mice	1,744,880	1,636,332	1,619,814
Pigs	8,650	8,801	8,584
Primates	5,280	5,284	3,630
Rabbits	113,370	89,845	43,824
Rats	882,256	891,235	873,058
Sheep	18,748	18,235	15,940

**Table 12. Experiments and Procedures on Living Animals
Northern Ireland[3]**

Categories	1989	1990
Total numbers of procedures on animals (incl. experiments)	15,215	
Number of procedures without anaesthetic (75.39%)	11,471	
Procedures on mice	2,182	
Procedures on rats	1,596	
Procedures on rabbits	2,003	
Procedures on carnivores	142	
Procedures on ungulates	2,352	
Procedures on birds	4,071	
Procedures on fish	2,476	statistics
Selection of medical and veterinary products	3,846	not
Animals used in toxicity testing - medical products	524	available
Animals used in toxicity testing - non-medical products	841	at time
Procedures deliberately causing psychological stress	129	of writing
Use of training stimuli	20	
Exposure to ionizing radiation	231	
Physical trauma to simulate injury	84	
LD50 & LC50	213	
Eye irritancy	4	
Skin irritancy	252	
Conducted by universities (incl. medical schools)	7,314	
Conducted by government departments	7,107	
Conducted by commercial concerns	794	
No. of visits to laboratories by inspectors	39	
No. of project licence holders	92	

8.

ZOOS

(See also **ANIMALS PERFORMING** chapter: similarities re animals in captivity. Close connections between circuses, zoos and safari parks. And **VIVISECTION** chapter: animal experiments conducted under zoo auspices and on animals from zoos).

Wild animals have been kept in private collections for '000s of years. The familiar type of zoo first began in 1765 when the Imperial Menagerie in Vienna was opened to the public.

General Information
During 1991, Zoo Directive by European Commission will lay down minimum conditions to be applied in all zoos in the EC (over 1,000, holding about 1m animals[1]). Zoos to be licensed by local authorities and subject to regular inspections of animals' physical and mental welfare. Some zoos will face closure.

In the UK, zoos are regulated by the Zoo Licensing Act 1981 which lays down minimum standards of zoo management; conditions are largely unspecified; no minimum amount of space for individual species; no minimum qualifications for zoo staff.

Zoo numbers UK. 1945: 14. 1951: 31. 1971: 131. (1984: Introduction of Zoo Licensing Act 1981). 1987: 198. About 30% hold mammals — approx. 30,000 individuals of about 150 species. Approx. 302 establishments in UK now exhibit animals, birds, reptiles or fish with a total of about 15m visitors/year. Animals are held as specimens. 50 of the UK institutions are represented by the National Federation of Zoological Gardens, based at London Zoo (one of the world's oldest) where the largest collection of species is held: about 139 species; 8,000 animals (mammals, birds, reptiles, amphibians, fish, spiders, insects).

In April 1991, the 15ha London Zoo which, along with the 250ha Whipsnade Zoo (2,800 animals), is run by the Institute of Zoology, announced imminent closure through lack of funds after being given £10m in 1988 by the government, its Regent's Park land-lord. Losses had been running at £2m/year. Opened in 1826 (opened to public in 1847), it was once Britain's most popular tourist attraction; now eighth. Annual visitors have fallen from 3m/year in the 1950s to 1.1m in 1990. By May 1991, Whipsnade was also under threat of closure. In June and July '91, private money was being offered to convert the Zoo into a conservation park, with up to 70% of the animals being distributed to other zoos and private collections.

Animals

Mostly born in captivity and/or received from other zoos. Some are still taken from the wild, separated from (often slaughtered) family, depleting natural stocks.

Barren cage environments; restrictive space (male tiger's terri-tory in wild extends up to 100km²); inappropriate design and con-struction (Marwell Zoo. 2 black rhinos died. Cage had to be cut to pieces to remove them). Solitary-living wild animals are kept in groups in zoos. Minimum or no privacy. Natural behaviours frustrated. Social structures destroyed or recreated artificially. Confinement is often increased in winter for many exotics. Some young, e.g. lion cubs, are separated from adults, hand-reared in pets' zoo for children to look at. Sticks and hooks are used to control animals. Some zoo animals have been trained to perform for the public, e.g. chimps tea party; walking on stilts; riding motor bikes.

Many zoo animals are destroyed due to incurable disease, injury, senility, surplus to requirements or inability to place in another collection. Animals have been shot or otherwise put down (e.g. overdose) when proving too difficult. Or transferred, sold to other zoos or circuses, following a pattern established with the UK's first zoo elephant, Jumbo who was sold to Barnum Circus in America in 1882 and was later hit and killed by a train whilst on tour in Canada.

Most of the dangerous zoo animals (carnivores and reptiles) were put down during the second world war to prevent mass escape in the blitz; others were evacuated to Whipsnade and

Dublin; others were eaten, whilst the Zoo undertook a large-scale rabbit-breeding programme to produce meat.[2]

Artificial insemination and breeding, genetic engineering and experimentation have been and are practised on zoo animals.

Until 1990, wallabies from Whipsnade were experimented upon at the Institute of Zoology (on London Zoo site), Regents Park, London. The work was funded by the Medical Research Council and the Agricultural and Food Research Council. (See VIVISECTION chapter).

Zoo animals are also sent out on 'breeding duty' to other zoos throughout the world.

Safari Parks. (World's first opened at Longleat in 1966). Animals share same problems of new climate, new feed, new diseases, new (artificial) social structure as zoo animals.

Dolphinaria (See ANIMALS PERFORMING chapter).

Troubles

Animals kept in captivity often become mentally ill, displaying stereotypic behaviour — rocking, swaying, compulsive grooming, rhythmic pacing, head-twisting/banging, weaving, mouthing, vomiting, self-mutilation, infanticide, bullying, territorial aggression. Frustration, distress. Helplessness, apathy, lethargy.

9 zoos in UK hold 20 polar bears (2-27 years in captivity). Over 50% suffer from abnormal behaviour patterns. 60-70% of cubs do not reach the age of one year. (10-30% in wild).[3] More elephants have died in zoos than have been born in them.

Lack of exercise. Susceptibility to disease. Skin complaints. Boredom. Heart attack. Foot rot. TB. Accident. Injury. Infant mortality. Premature death. Parasites. Cowpox. Unwanted interbreeding.

Appendix A: *ILLEGAL CRUELTY* [1]

Table 13. RSPCA Inspectorate Statistics (England & Wales)		
Convictions	**1989**	**1990**
Cruelty to dogs	1,131	1,512
Dog fighting[†]	19	62
Cruelty to cats	214	191
Cruelty to horses, donkeys	51	149
Cruelty to cattle, sheep, pigs	198	316*
Offences under Wildlife &		
Countryside Act	149	162*
Casework		
Complaints investigated	82,948	85,867
Convictions (see above)	2,026	2,608
Cautions issued	4,849	4,229
Prison sentences	28	44
Suspended prison sentences	16	9
Juvenile offenders	11	3
Disqualification orders	715	856
Rescues	2,768	2,530
Inspections undertaken	18,516	16,936
Phone calls to Inspectorate	1,053,360	1,162,219
*sheep 168; wild birds 135; cattle 109; rabbits 66; pigs 39; goats 27; badgers 27; domestic fowl 23; snakes 22.		
Maximum fine for cruelty to animals in England and Wales is £2,000, rising to £5,000 when Criminal Justice Bill is approved.		

[†] Dogfighting. Held in makeshift 'pit'. Run in accordance with rules, with referee and timekeeper. If neither dog killed, loser is dog which refuses to cross 'scratch line' to continue fight. Training techniques include weight-training, treadmills and use of cats and dogs as bait. Ears may be removed by amateurs and without anaesthetic. Powerful clinical drugs used at fights. Breeds: American Pit Bull Terrier, Staffordshire and English Bull Terriers.

Table 14. Scottish SPCA Statistics		
	1988/89	**1990/91**
Investigations	3,386	3,899
(88/89: Some 5,000 sheep were found to be neglected to a degree)		
Verbal cautions issued	862	709
Written cautions issued	5	6
Proceedings taken		
Concerning domestic animals	82	69*
Concerning farm animals	25	24
Concerning wildlife**	6	4
Resulting in		
Fines	82	55*
Imprisonments	2	4*
Admonishments	16	21
Bans		31

* Plus sentences imposed on 31 people involved in dog-fighting in Fife. Offenders all sentenced with total fines of £11,750 and 52 months imprisonment.

** Wild birds, and in particular the finch species, are still under threat from those who indulge in trapping them with the use of birdlime. The idea is to cross breed these birds with a canary to produce a mule or hybrid for show purposes. Very few survive in captivity. (SSPCA Annual Report 1990).

Maximum fine for cruelty to animals in Scotland is £1,000, rising to £2,500 when Criminal Justice Bill approved.

In Britain in 1989, seven successful cases were brought by MAFF which also assisted local authorities and the police in bringing 92 successful cases and other bodies in bringing a further 11 successful cases.[1] (Farm Animals).

The destruction of pets, e.g. drowning kittens by 'owners', could be regarded as an offence under the Protection of Animals Act 1911, the Protection of Animals (Scotland) Act 1912, the Animal Welfare Act (N. Ireland) 1972.

Table 15. Ulster SPCA Statistics (N. Ireland)
1.1.89 - 31.3.90 (1990/91 figures X at time of writing).

Convictions

Cruelty to

dogs	21	(46 dogs involved)
badgers/set damage	4*	
cats	2**	
cattle	2	
rooks	1	
donkey	1	
pony	1	
finches	1	
horse	1	
sheep	1	

* and ** each include also one of the dog cruelty convictions.

Casework

Convictions	33
Complaints investigated	2023
Dogfighting, badger-baiting investigations	28

Table 16. Aberdeen APCA Statistics

Improper Treatment	1989	1990
Horses & ponies	2	2
Destroyed	0	2
Cattle	1	2
Destroyed	0	1
Sheep	0	4
Destroyed	2	1
Pigs	0	0
Destroyed	0	0
Dogs	1	6
Destroyed	See Pets Table	
Cats	2	3
Destroyed	See Pets Table	

Appendix B: *BSE*

Bovine Spongiform Encephalopathy (BSE) was first discovered in 1986. "This country, more than any other in the world, is a nation of milk drinkers. To fulfil that need we had to give cows a lot of animal protein to supplement their normal diets. That is why sheep carcases were fed to cattle."[1]

The sheep offal contaminated with scrapie, a brain-related disease that has been present in Britain for at least 250 years, was to possibly to blame. Similar diseases have been found in other animals, including zoo antelopes, domestic cats and laboratory mice fed on infected meat. Humans suffer from a related illness, Creutzfeldt-Jakob disease, and 4,000 Papua New Guinea tribespeople are believed to have contracted an even rarer disease, kuru, through cannibalism.

France banned imports of all British beef from 30.5.90 due to fears of BSE. Earlier, EC countries and other nations stopped importing live British cattle more than 6 months old. France was the biggest market for British beef exports in 1989 and accounted for about half of sales worldwide. BSE killed about 13,000 British cows May'86-May'90. They had been given fodder containing contaminated sheep offal.[2]

In July 1988 a ban was imposed on the feeding of sheep protein to cattle. In December the government banned the sale of milk from infected cows as a 'precautionary measure'.[3]

At the height of the BSE scare the Meat & Livestock Commission launched a £1.2m advertising campaign persuading people to eat meat. Beef accounts for half of all meat consumption. 95% of Britons eat meat but they eat less than in any other European country apart from Portugal.[4]

Cases of 'mad cow' disease, which has killed 17,489 cattle on 8,723 farms and is still (July 1991) running at 300 a week, will not fall significantly until 1992; the epidemic will affect herds until the end of the decade.[5]

The appearance of BSE has led to animals being used in research to find the BSE agent.

BSE Timetable[6]

1732. Scrapie first recorded in sheep.

Late 1970s/early 1980s. Rendering techniques for sheep offal change (fat-removing solvents no longer used), and sheep population starts rapid rise.

April 1985. First signs of new cattle disease.

November 1986. BSE identified.

April 1988. Southwood Committee set up.

June 1988. BSE made a notifiable disease.

July 1988. Government bans use of ruminant protein in ruminant feed.

August 1988. Compulsory slaughter introduced with 50% compensation. All suspect carcases incinerated or buried and not allowed to enter food chain.

December 1988. Government bans sale of milk from BSE suspects.

January 1989. First BSE case reported in Ireland.

February 1989. Southwood report published: human risks remote. New BSE (Tyrrell) committee set up.

November 1989. Ban on use as feed of bovine spleen, spinal cord, brain, thymus, tonsils and intestines from UK slaughtered cattle.

January 1990. Tyrrell Report published. Government to spend £12m in next three years on BSE research.

February 1990. Farmers to get 100% compensation.

May 1990. Cat infected with BSE in laboratory experiment. Beef consumption falls by 45%.

September 1990. Pig infected with BSE in laboratory experiment. Government bans feeding selected offal (as above) to all animals, including pets.

October 1990. Two cases of suspected mad cow type disease reported at London Zoo affecting an Arabian oryx and a greater kudu after being fed diet of commercial dairy pellets which were known to contain a high proportion of protein derived from sheep.

November 1990. MAFF announces inquiry into practices of animal foodstuff industry.

December 1990. Official figures show that 21,000 cattle, mostly dairy animals, died from BSE since 1985. In 1990, 18 BSE animals were buried on-farm. Figure likely to increase as knackermen now charging to take carcases away.

January 1991. BSE figure rises to over 22,000. Article in *The Lancet* warns that farm burial of cattle with mad cow disease should cease immediately, claiming that the virus is virtually indestructable in typical soil conditions.

February 1991. A record 1,515 cases confirmed in month.

March 1991. First case of 'mad calf' disease involving a 26-month-old dairy cow —
5 months pregnant — born after the November 1988 ban on scrapie-infected sheep
offals being used as cattle feed. Total number of deaths rises to 26,000 (in 11,000
herds) with another 26,000 expected in 1991.

April 1991. MAFF scientists suspect that BSE may be an independent, specifically
cattle disease, caused by feeding of BSE-infected brains of previously slaughtered
cows. MAFF records show that affected cattle have typically been fed more beef
offals than sheep offals. Deaths reach almost 27,000.

July 1991. Agriculture select committee report accuses the government of 'dangerous complacency' over a 'serious environmental problem'. Nearly half of the 1.5m
dead animals normally collected by knackermen are being buried on farms with
a steady incidence of cattle being left by the side of the road with their ear tags
removed and dead sheep being found floating in rivers.

1996. Southwood predicted BSE starting to disappear, but this predicted before
April 1991 suspicions.

Appendix C: *EXPORT-IMPORT*

Farm Animals

Farm animals are transported from the UK across Europe to slaughter (and for breeding or fattening). Journeys can last over 24 hours, as far as into Italy, with little or no food and water. Many animals die in transit, from exhaustion, trampling, heat, cold. Shipping fever — a respiratory health problem — can occur within 6-8 hours of departure. Problems arise also from pre-transport handling; unsuitable facilities; unsuitable design and construction of vehicles; inadequate inspection; difficulties in enforcing legislation. Animals are often transported long distances to countries paying maximum sale price.

At present, horses and ponies are supposedly not exported live for slaughter (only for show and breeding, but see figures below), being prevented by Minimum Values Act 1969 making import of equines uneconomic, and by Animals Health Act 1981. New European law from 1992 may demand that horse trade recommence and may mean export of live animals over distances of 8,000km to Saudi Arabia, for instance.

Most of the bull calves exported live to Europe are reared for veal, often in veal crates, with their 'white' flesh often being imported back into the UK for the catering trade.

In July 1989, the UK was prohibited by the EC from sending to other member states live cattle born before 18 July 1988 or which are the offspring of dams affected by BSE.

In July 1990 a 'commando group' of French farmers poisoned 94 of a consignment of 206 British sheep with insecticide. In August 1990, French farmers set fire to a livestock lorry carrying 439 British sheep, burning 219 to death; the rest had to be destroyed due to burns. In the same month, live sheep were also used by the French farmers as 'battering rams' against police shields during demonstrations against British imports. On 6 September, more than 300 Scottish lambs were slaughtered and their carcases burned on the streets of Bellac. Further hi-jacks followed.[1]

Exports of live sheep from the UK to France soared by 242% in 1990. From January to March 1989, France imported 46,300 live sheep from the UK. In the same period 1990, France imported 158,700 lambs from the UK.[2]

Table 17. Live Export — Farm Animals & Fish[4] (Numbers, unless stated)			
	1989		**1990**
Cattle	329,517		351,501
(incl. calves	278,215	male	312,623
	41,086	female	33,177)
Breeding stock	4,355		8,803)
Sheep	589,336		584,005
(incl. breeding stock	1,187		2,186)
Goats	195		335
Pigs	114,783		131,582
(incl. breeding stock	17,248		23,345)
Poultry (all types)	13,554,891		14,645,547
Horses	7,399		7,483
(incl. for slaughter	104		21)
Asses, mules, hinnies	80		23
Rabbits	3,752		1,572
Pigeons	996		1,073
Others	1,368 t		1,133 t
Ornamental fish (fresh water)	67,116kg		79,887kg
Ornamental fish (salt water)	13,334kg		24,282kg
Trout	21,008kg		21,348kg
Eels	473,799kg		312,751kg
Carp	290kg		3,110kg
Salmon	5,572kg		20,850kg
Others	27,420kg		12,288kg
Saltwater fish	47,455kg		39,168kg
Total fish	656 t		514 t

During 1989, 52.3m hatching eggs were exported from the UK. Semen and embryos are routinely exported and imported. Bovine semen is exported to about 35 countries and porcine semen to six.[3]

Table 18. Live Import — Farm Animals & Fish[4] (Numbers, unless stated)			
	1989		1990
Cattle	123,600		124,692
(incl. Calves	633	male	351
	20	female	4)
Sheep	102,923		119,217
Goats	484		128
Pigs	56,982		52,581
Poultry	2,459,770		3,224,583
Horses	10,917		10,418
(incl. for slaughter	7		13)
Asses, mules, hinnies	1		19
Rabbits	2,241		410
Pigeons	38,175		2,807
Others	456 t		421 t
Ornamental fish (fresh water)	887,457kg		1,066,957kg
Ornamental fish (salt water)	265,100kg		204,377kg
Trout	—		—
Eels	191,865kg		217,754kg
Carp	143,391kg		129,192kg
Salmon	571kg		—
Others	1,339kg		13,756kg
Saltwater fish	180kg		31,178kg
Total fish (mostly from Israel, Singapore, Japan and USA).	1,490 t		1,663 t

Wild Animals

The major control over traffic in wildlife is the Convention on the International Trade in Endangered Species (CITES), also known as the Washington Convention, which came into effect in 1975. 110 countries belong to CITES, many notorious for failing to enforce the treaty, e.g. Spain, Thailand, Argentina, Soviet Union, Indonesia. Many countries not signatory, e.g. Burma, Cambodia, Laos, Sierra Leone, Yugoslavia, Mexico. Species are listed under Appendices I, II or III.

I: Species threatened with extinction. Includes chimps, gorillas, orang-utangs, cheetahs, tigers, rhinos. Trade banned (exemption for 'scientific purposes' means '000s of exotics going into labs and zoos each year). The chimpanzee is threatened with extinction in the wild because thousands are captured for Aids research experiments. About 2,000 were sold in 1990. Zoologists estimate 10 die for every one that reaches the lab. Up to 20,000 died in 1990 from a total wild population of 150,000.[5]

II: Species potentially threatened by trade. Trade permitted if officially authorized by country of origin as not detrimental to species survival. Includes bottlenose dolphins. 100,000s of primates/year traded thus for research labs.

III: Animals considered worthy of protection. Listed by country of origin.

Loophole in CITES allows captive-born individuals of species on Appendix I to be traded as though they belonged to Appendix II.

1988-90. 9,588 wild monkeys taken from natural habitats and used for experimentation purposes in Britain.

Imported captive birds. In 1989, 184,600 birds were imported; 4,000 of them dead on arrival, a further 19,500 died in post-import quarantine. Average mortality 12-14%. Mortality in some species is 50-100%. Of 364 hanging parrots imported in 1989, more than three-quarters died. Of 121 crested mynahs imported, only 36 lived with 22 dead and 63 dying in quarantine. Argentina shipped 153 Monk parakeets to the UK in 1989; 3 were dead on arrival and 117 died in quarantine. Shipping conditions poor, e.g. 50 parrots in a 0.9 x 0.45 x 0.22m crate.[6] Of 47 humming birds imported from Peru in 1988, 21 were already dead and the rest perished in quarantine. Of 280 honey creepers imported via the Netherlands, 68 were dead and 194 died later.[7] No figures available on birds dying at time of or just after capture from wild in native countries. Maximum non-parrot (non-psittacine) species in any consignment permitted in any licence issued from 1 April 1991 has been reduced from 6,000 to 4,000. Many of the problems with this trade would be reduced if the public no longer purchased captive birds.[8]

Millions of animals are removed from the world's forests each year, exported to end up in zoos, circuses, labs etc. or as pets or as food. Majority die before reaching destination.

In the year to March 1990 customs officers seized 1,546 illegally imported live wild animals, including 571 lizards, 533 birds, 171 snakes, 90 turtles, 50 toads, 48 tortoises, 40 frogs, 22 parrots, 12 salamanders, 8 monkeys and 1 feline.[9] In 1988, licences for the import of almost 500m ornamental fish were issued.[10]

Table 19. Customs & Excise Seizures of Live Animals and Prosecutions under UK Conservation Controls[11]

1989	Numbers seized	1990
239	reptiles, amphibians	1,567
47	birds	744 + 12 eggs (export)
3	mammals	8

Prosecutions:

Number of offenders 5.
Total fines £2,100 plus
one sentence of 6 months
suspended for 2 years.
Costs awarded £1,550.

Number of offenders 5.
Total fines £1,000 plus 3
prison sentences totalling 63
months.

**Table 20. Raw Furskins (i.e. not incl. tanned, dressed furs*).
Import[4] (Numbers unless stated)**

1989		1990
2,967,180	Mink	1,482,769
83,302	Rabbit, hare	88,216
569,664	Lamb***	11,022
12,010	Beaver	15,305
353,107	Muskrat	133,323
383,117	Fox	124,611
1,193	Seal	6,400
2,601	Sea otter, Nutria^	51,229
100	Marmots	2,100
4,500	Wild feline	—
37,107kg	Others	49,152kg

* Approx 100,000 in 1990.
*** Astrakan, Persian etc. ^ S. American coypu

Table 21. Import. Miscellaneous Selection from CITES Statistics 1989 (Latest available)[12]

App.			
II	Indian macaque tissue cultures		8,695
II	Vervet or green monkey tissue cultures		7,379
II	African elephant skin pieces	(min.)	2,822m^2
II	Alligator meat		1,939kg
II	Alligator watchstraps		10,200
II	Caiman crocodilus crocodilus skins		4,002
II	Caiman crocodilus crocodilus watchstraps		32,131*
II	Tupinambis teguixin (lizard) skins		27,040
II	Varanus niloticus (Nile monitor) skins		25,397
	ditto	watchstraps	9558
II	Varanus salvator (lizard) skins		218,135
	ditto	skin pieces	10,000
	ditto	watchstraps	53,185
II	Python reticulatus skins		85,827
III	Pytas mucosus (Indian rat snake) handbags		11,787
	ditto	pairs of shoes	43,237
	ditto	skins	320,397

* Items from other crocodile species also imported.

Ivory

9 October 1989, Lausanne. African elephant raised to CITES Appendix 1 status thus banning international trade in ivory. To be reviewed in 1991. Slaughter of these animals for ivory left orphaned calves, many of whom were taken for circuses.

Feed

Europe imports 14m tonnes of the 3rd World's harvest each year to feed to its farmed animals. In 1990, the UK imported over 4m tonnes of animal feed (excl. unmilled cereals).

Appendix D: *UK EXOTICS*

(Further information on exotic animals will be found in the **COUNTRY SPORTS, FUR ANIMALS, ANIMALS PERFORMING, PETS, & ZOOS** chapters).

Animals which have been introduced (or re-introduced ike the European beaver and wild boar, both native to Britain until exterminated in 12th and 17th centuries respectively) outside of their normal range, deliberately or inadvertently. At least 76 species involved. Held for 7 main reasons: display to paying public (e.g. zoos); performance (e.g. circuses and cabaret); sale in shops; quarantine; research purposes; commercial breeding for pelts or flesh (incl. wild boar); as pets or part of collection.

Most recent (1989; ADAS and DoE) figures showed that under the Dangerous Wild Animals Act 1976, 726-955 animals of at least 76 species were held under 177 licences. Most popular group: New-World monkeys, especially squirrel monkeys (about 33%). Raccoons are the most frequently-kept carnivores. Greatest numbers of such animals are held in zoos and wildlife parks.

Those which have escaped or been released into wild and formed established populations over the centuries are: coypu; edible dormouse; Chinese water deer; Fallow deer; muntjac deer; sika deer; mink; house mouse; muskrat; Himalayan porcupine; rabbit; common rat; ship rat; grey squirrel; red-necked wallaby.

Between January 1970 and October 1989, over 293 exotic mammals, of at least 39 species not normally kept as household pets, were recorded out of captivity on 127 occasions. 62% were recaptured; 17% suffered an unknown fate; 12% were shot; 4% were road casualties; 3% died in other accidents; 2% fell victim to dogs and cats.[1]

Zander fish, which can grow up to 0.6m long, introduced into the Norfolk Broads in the 1950s, have now spread and thrive in the Midlands canal system. Numbers are reduced — about 100-150/year — by British Waterways electro-fishing. Electric current sent through water to stun fish which float to surface. Zander sold to local restaurants or Billingsgate fish market.[2]

Appendix E: *CAMELIDS*

General

Originated in the Americas. Several UK herds of 10-20 animals, research stations having more; approx. 100 in all. Few farms, most animals found on odd hectares about the countryside. Main output: breeding animals and/or fibre. Possible development of male llamas for driving, trekking and as pets.

Breeding

Species farmed in UK: Llama glama, Llama guanaco, Llama pacos (alpaca). Pure breeding encouraged. Offspring tend to be kept or sold privately.

Llama glama. Females mature at 18 months, males at 2-3 years. Surplus males culled. No regular breeding season in UK. Ovulation induced. Gestation period 11 months. Single calf, twins rare.

Alpacas gestation 11-12 months. Single calf, twins rare. Mated again 10-15 days after calving. 50% of embryos die within 1st month. Mated again.

Guanacos. Wild animals. Local authority licence needed. Females mature at 2, males at 3. Gestation 11 months, single calf.

At the Rowett Research Institute there are 50 llamas, alpacas and guacanos. Embryo recovery and superovulation successfully developed.

A research programme is under way at the Welsh Plant Breeding Station, Aberystwyth, and the Institute of Zoology in London, hoping to cross vicuna with guanaco if negotiations lead to permission to import embryos from S. America.

Housing

Usually outdoors but shelter essential. Unlike sheep, coats do not contain lanolin. Males usually removed from herd and paddocked individually. Space essential, especially for guanaco.

Feeding

Grazing and browsing plus hay and concentrates, as for sheep, goats.

Output

Wool from the llama sells for 2-3 times price of sheep wool. The fibre from the rarer alpaca 3-4 times, and guanaco undercoat 60-70 times.

Llama glama. Fleece black, brown, grey, white or combination. Sheared annually or bi-annually. Average yield 1.4-3.2kg/year. Very soft yarn produced by de-hairing, removing rough outer coat.

Alpaca fleece brown, black, sometimes white, grey and chestnut. Sheared annually, often sedated. Lack of natural grease means shears become burning hot. Air-cooled clippers preferable. Superior quality to llama. Yield 2.2-5kg/year.

Guanaco fleece brown. Often sedated for clipping. Twin fibre, rough and smooth, latter accounting for 80%. Yield 1.3-2.2kg/year.

Diseases
Clostridial disease. Worms.

Appendix F: *SNAILS*

Breeder boxes hold about 20-25 breeders, each producing up to 40 eggs/week.

Once hatched, growers kept, for instance, 500-5000 in 1.2 x 0.6m plastic trays in sheds; high temperatures (around 27°C) to prevent hibernation. 4 months old at sale. (Free-range system allows hibernation, snails taking about 18 months to reach edible size). Fast-growing and giant species now bred.

Feeding. Compound (e.g sow breeder meal) plus limestone flour, powdered milk and concentrate feed. Or outdoor grazing in pens; mesh tunnels.

Sold live to restaurants etc. Killed by boiling in water, or immersing in brine for 24-36 hours.

Appendix G: *LAWS*

The selected Acts (Statutes), Orders and Regulations (Statutory Instruments) listed chronologically below cover the main UK legislation relating to animals and their welfare. No attempt has been made (or has been possible for this publication) to detail each piece of legislation, but brief notes are appended to some whilst others should, in this context, need no more explanation than their titles imply. Further details of certain major legislation are included earlier in relevant chapters. Acts under which Orders and Regulations are made are shown italicized in parentheses at the end of an entry. (A.H.A.) refers to the Animal Health Acts; (R) refers to laws which have been repealed (replaced by later legislation).

1822. **Act to Prevent the Cruel & Improper Treatment of Cattle.** 'Martin's Act' (Richard 'Humanity Dick' Martin MP). First national law in the world dealing specifically with cruelty to animals. (R).

1828. **The Night Poaching Act.**

1831. **The Game Act.** Close seasons etc.

1835 **Act** (Joseph Pease MP) outlawing animal baiting and fighting, and amending the 1822 Act. (R).

1843. **Pound Breach Act.**

1849. **Prevention of Cruelty Act.** (R).

1847. **The Town Police Clauses Act.** Police powers re offences involving animals; including baiting and dogfighting.

1848. **The Hares Act.** Prohibiting shooting at night.

1854. Prohibition on use of carts drawn by dogs. (R).

1860. **The Game Licences Act.** Making some licences necessary.

1862. **The Poaching Prevention Act.** Police powers.

1869. **Sea Birds Protection Act.** Protection during nesting seasons.

1871. **The Dogs Act.** Courts' powers re dog owners. Amended by Dangerous Dogs Act 1989.

1875. **The Seal Fishery Act.** Specifying prohibited areas and seasons.

1876. **The Cruelty to Animals Act.** Vivisection. (R). Superseded by Animals (Scientific Procedures) Act 1986.

1878. **Animals in Transit Act.** (R).

1880. **The Ground Game Act.** Re landowners killing hares, rabbits.

1883. **Customs and Inland Revenue Act.**

1887. Pit ponies protection.

1892. **The Hares Preservation Act**. Prohibiting sale of hares, leverets March-July.

1894. **The Behring Sea Award Act**. GB-USA agreement re seals.

1894-1935. **The Diseases of Animals Acts.**

1895. **The Seal Fisheries (North Pacific) Act**. Re seals, otters and others.

1900. **Wild Animals in Captivity Protection Act**. (R).

1904. Pole Trap banned. (R).

1906. **The Dogs Act**. Stray dogs. Police powers and responsibilities. Prohibiting transfer of strays to laboratories.

1906. **The Ground Game (Amendment) Act**. Hares.

1908. Hooking wild birds prohibited. (R).

1910. Restriction on transportation of horses (Diseases of Animals Bill). (R).

1911. **The Protection of Animals Act.**

1912. **The Protection of Animals (Scotland) Act**. Principal statutes relating to protection of domestic and captive animals. Forbidding acts of cruelty or the causing of unnecessary suffering to any animal (other than wild animals).

The 1911 Act was repealed (though not entirely) in N. Ireland by the Animal Welfare Act 1972.

1912. **The Seal Fisheries (North Pacific) Act**. Re seals, otters and others.

1914. Strengthening the 1910 horse transportation legislation. (R).

1919. **The Conveyance of Live Poultry Order**. (Diseases of Animals Acts 1894-35; Animal Health Act 1981).

1923. **The Salmon and Freshwater Fisheries Act.**

1925. **The Performing Animals (Regulations) Act**. Circuses etc. Local Authority registration, powers; police powers. No control of conditions in which animals are kept.

1927. **The Transit of Animals Order**. (*A.H.A. 1981*). (R).

1928. **The Dogs (Amendment) Act**. Stray dogs. Police powers, responsibilities.

1930. **The Animals (Sea Transport) Order**. (*A.H.A. 1981*).

1931. **The Improvement of Livestock (Licensing of Bulls) Act.**

1932. **The Destructive Imported Animals Act** and its Orders. Prohibiting the keeping of certain animals — muskrats, mink, musquash, grey squirrels and other non-indigenous species. Precautions against escape. (And see 1982 & 1987).

1933. **The Slaughter of Animals Act**. Introduced pre-slaughter stunning. (R).

1933. **The Protection of Animals (Cruelty to Dogs) Act**. Disqualifications of convicted persons.

1934. **The Protection of Animals Act**. Making bullfights and aspects of rodeos illegal.

1934. **The Whaling Industry (Regulation) Act.** Prohibiting capture of cetaceans within 200 miles of British coast.

1936. **Public Health Act.**

1937. **The Poultry (Exposure for Sale) Order.** (*Diseases of A. A. 1894-35; A.H.A. 1981*).

1937. **The Cinematograph Films (Animals) Act.** Prohibiting cruelty to animals in filming and the showing of films directed as to cause cruelty to the animals involved.

1937. **The Diseases of Fish Act.** Re importation of live fish and fish eggs.

1938. **The Dogs Amendment Act.** Re destruction of dangerous dogs.

1939. **The Prevention of Damage by Rabbits Act.** Re killing of wild rabbits.

1946. **Hill Farming Act.**

1947. **The Agriculture Act.** Husbandry management guide. Prevention of escape. Pests control.

1948. **The Veterinary Act.**

1949. **The Slaughter of Animals (Scotland) Act.**

1949. **The Docking and Nicking of Horses Act.** Prohibiting both practices. Veterinary exemptions.

1949. **The Prevention of Damage by Pests Act.** Personal and local authority responsibilities.

1950. **Minimum Values Order** (amended by the Ponies Act 1969). (*A.H.A. 1981*).

1950. **Diseases of Animals Act.** (R).

1950. **The Dogs Act.** (R).

1951. **The Livestock Rearing Act.** Re seizure and sale of rams and lambs, ref. Hill Farming Act 1946.

1951. **Salmon and Freshwater Fisheries (Protection) (Scotland) Act.**

1951-83. **The Pet Animals Acts.** Licensing pet shops. Prohibiting sale of animals as pets in street, market stall etc. No sale of animals to children under 12.

1952. **The Cockfighting Act.** Prohibiting possession of cockfighting instruments.

1952. **The Agriculture (Poisonous Substances) Act.** Some animal experiments conducted to satisfy this.

1953. **The Dogs (Protection of Livestock) Act.** Re dogs worrying livestock on agricultural land.

1954. **The Agriculture (Miscellaneous Provisions) Act.**

1954. **The Pests Act.** Clearance of rabbits. Banning certain traps as from 1958.

1954. **The Protection of Birds Act.** Making it an offence to keep a bird in a cage which is too small to allow the bird to spread its wings fully. The Act excludes poultry from such protection. (R).

1954. The Slaughter of Animals (Pigs) Act. Made compulsory the mechanical stunning of pigs slaughtered outside abattoirs. Many reared and killed in back yards at the time. (R).

1954. The Protection of Animals (Anaesthetics) Act. Mainly re surgical procedures on livestock. Operations under the Animals (Scientific Procedures) Act 1986 are excluded.

1955. The Food and Drugs Act. Some animal experiments conducted to satisfy.

1957. The Agriculture Act.

1958. The Slaughter of Pigs (Anaesthesia) Regulations. (*Slaughter of Animals Act 1933 and 1954; Slaughterhouses Act 1958; now Slaughterhouses Act 1974*).

1958. The Slaughter of Animals (Prevention of Cruelty) Regulations. Refers to ability of slaughterman and condition of equipment. (*As above except S.A.A. 1933*).

1958. The Horse Breeding Act. Licensing of stallions.

1959. The Deer (Scotland) Act. Red Deer Commission set up. Introduction of (shooting) close seasons as from 1962.

1959. The Dog Licences Act.

1960. The Abandonment of Animals Act. Prohibiting.

1960. The Game Laws (Amendment) Act.

1961. The Public Health Act. Local authority killing of birds in built-up areas.

1962. The Animals (Cruel Poisons) Act. Refers to incidental killing of non-target animals.

1962. The Veterinary Surgery (Exemptions) Order. Refers to surgical procedures, mutilations on animals before and after certain ages. (*Veterinary Act 1948*).

1963. The Deer Act. Close seasons.

1963. The Animal Boarding Establishments Act. Conditions and licensing re boarding of cats and dogs only.

1963-1980. The Deer Acts (and see below). Close seasons, methods of killing. Deer kept commercially within deer-proof enclosures not covered by the Acts.

1964. The Protection of Animals (Anaesthetics) Act . Mainly re surgical procedures on livestock. Operations under the Animals (Scientific Procedures) Act 1986 are excluded.

1964. The Riding Establishments Act. Licensing, conditions, care of equines.

1964. Markets (Protection of Animals) Order. Intending protection of animals at or to and from markets. (*A.H.A. 1981*). (R).

1966. The Veterinary Surgeons Act. Refers to surgical procedures, mutilations on animals before and after certain ages. Registration of vets; prohibitions on unqualified persons.

1966. The Fisheries (N. Ireland) Act.

1967. **The Agriculture Act.**

1967. **The Diseases of Fish (N. Ireland) Act.**

1967. **The Sea Fisheries (Shellfish) Act.**

1967. **The Deer (Amendment) (Scotland) Act.**

1967. **The Forestry Act.** Forestry Commission powers re killing tree-damaging species of animal.

1967. **The Slaughter of Poultry Act.** Slaughterhouse registration. Refers to protection whilst awaiting slaughter. Making compulsory the manual back-up to the automatic knife. Exemptions for Muslim and Jewish slaughter. (And see Animal Health & Welfare Act 1984).

1968. **The Agriculture (Miscellaneous Provisions) Act.** Principal statute relating specifically to the welfare of farm animals. Enacted as a response to the Brambell Report (1965) from the Technical Committee appointed by the UK Government after publication of Ruth Harrison's *Animal Machines* (Vincent Stuart 1964). Forbids the causing of unnecessary pain or unnecessary stress to any livestock. Prohibits or restricts certain practices, e.g. hot branding of cattle. Also empowers Ministers to prepare codes of practice regarding livestock welfare (See below).

1968. **The Firearms Act.**

1968. **The Medicines Act.** Regulating drug licensing. Animal experiments.

1968. **The Theft Act.**

1969. **Export of Horses (Protection) Order.** Conditions, and restricting the permitted size of horses leaving the country. (*A.H.A. 1981*).

1969. **Minimum Values Act.** Re live equine export.

1969. **The Ponies Act.** See 1950. (R).

1970. **The Agriculture Act.**

1970. **The Conservation of Seals Act.** Grey and common seals. Close seasons; prohibitions on certain methods; fisherman's exemptions, licences.

1970. **The Riding Establishment Act.** Licensing, conditions, care of equines. Deals with less than full licence under 1964 Act (see above).

1971. **The Animals Act.** Damage by animals. Killing of dogs worrying livestock.

1971. **The Wild Creatures and Forest Laws Act.**

1972. **The Welfare of Animals Act.** N. Ireland only. Main animal welfare provisions in that country. Repealed (though not in its entirety) the Protection of Animals Act 1911.

1972. **The Agriculture (Miscellaneous Provisions) Act.** Re poisons for killing squirrels and coypus.

1972. **The Road Traffic Act.** Responsibilities of persons involved with road accidents with animals.

1973. The Transit of Animals (General) Order. Amended by The Transit of Animals (Amendment) Order 1988. Covers all animals carried by sea, air, road, rail. (*A.H.A. 1981*).

1973. The Badgers Act. Prohibiting cruelty, killing, digging, selling, marking, possession. Exemptions. Police powers.

1973. The Breeding of Dogs Act. Licensing premises where more than 2 bitches are kept for breeding for sale.

1974. The Health & Safety at Work Act. Some animal experiments conducted to satisfy this.

1974. The Slaughterhouses Act. Licensing. All animals to be stunned prior to slaughter. Exclusion clause for animals slaughtered for Muslim and Jewish communities by a licensed person of either faith. Religious (ritual) slaughter exempted from need to use stunning before slaughter. Since 1908, Jewish ritual method — shechita — permitted (performed by Jewish slaughterman [Shochet] licensed by Chief Rabbi). Since 1933 (1928 in Scotland) Muslim ritual method — halal — permitted. No such licensing or training. Adopted by EEC 1974. Member countries free to prohibit.

1974. The Welfare of Livestock (Regulations) Act.

1974. The Docking of Pigs (Use of Anaesthetics) Order. (*Protection of Animals [Anaesthetics] Act 1954; Agriculture [Miscellaneous Provisions] Act 1968*).

1974. The Rabies (Importation of Dogs, Cats and Other Mammals) Order. To control spread of disease. (*A.H.A. 1981*).

1975. The Transit of Animals (Road and Rail) Order. Forbidding excessive use of 'any instrument or thing used for driving the animal' whilst (un)loading, forbidding use of vehicles which could cause injury or suffering due to exposure, inadequate fresh air etc. Animals must be offered food and water at least every 12 hours during the journey - unless the journey can be completed within 15 hours of their last feed. Forbids transport of any animal if 'by reason of its unfitness, the animal is likely to be subjected to unnecessary suffering' or may give birth. Enforced by the local authority.

1975. The Farriers (Registration) Act. Powers and function of Farriers Registration Council.

1975. The Guard Dogs Act. Regulations re use.

1975. The Spring Traps (Approval) Order. (*Protection of Animals Act 1911; Pests Act 1954*).

1975. The Salmon and Freshwater Fisheries Act. Close seasons; licensing.

1975. The Conservation of Wild Creatures and Wild Plants Act. (R).

1976. The Freshwater and Salmon Fisheries (Scotland) Act.

1976. The Dangerous Wild Animals Act, and Modification Order 1984. Licensing. Restrictions on keeping large exotic wild animals. Zoos, circuses, pet shops and labs exempted.

1976. The Endangered Species (Import and Export) Act. Prohibits export-import of listed animals. Protection of endangered species and birds eggs. Implements Britain's obligations under the Convention on International Trade in Endangered Species of Wild Fauna and Flora (CITES: 1973/5).

1977. The Slaughter of Poultry Acts (Humane Conditions) Regulations. (*Slaughter of Poultry Act 1967*).

1977. The Roe Deer (Close Seasons) Act.

1978. Otter protection. England.

1978. Killing of Seals (Scotland). Prohibition. Exemptions.

1978. The Welfare of Livestock (Intensive Units) Regulations. Re inspection of livestock and equipment.

1979. The Transit of Animals Order. (*A.H.A. 1981*).

1980. The Deer Act. Re unlawful entry onto land to pursue deer. Venison records.

1980. The Removal of Antlers in Velvet (Anaesthetics) Order. (*Agriculture [Miscellaneous Provisions] Act 1968*).

1980. The Veterinary Surgeons Act 1966 (Schedule 3 Amendment) Order.

1980. The Welfare of Livestock (Deer) Regulations. (*Agriculture [Miscellaneous Provisions] Act 1968*).

1980. The Import of Live Fish (England & Wales) Act.

1981. The Animal Health Act. Control, eradication of disease. Notifiable diseases. Live animal transport; export and import. Restricting export of horses and ponies.

1981. The Diseases of Animals (N. Ireland) Order. Along with the Welfare of Animals Act 1972, covers main animal welfare provisions in N. Ireland.

1981. The Wildlife and Countryside Act. Replacing various Protection of Birds Acts. Protection for certain wild animals (including cetaceans) and birds, and birds in captivity (except poultry). Prohibition of self-locking snares (but not of free-running snare), poisons, nets, bows, live animal decoys. Makes offence of release of non-indigenous animals into wild (incl. fish, but with exemptions).

1981. Otter protection. Scotland.

1981. The Fisheries Act.

1981. The Zoo Licensing Act. Came into operation 1984. Licenses establishments where animals on exhibition to public for more than 7 days in any 12 months. Circuses and pet shops excluded.

1981. The Export of Animals (Protection) Order. (*A.H.A. 1981*).

1982. The Mink (Keeping) Order, made under the 1932 Act. Prohibiting keeping of mink except under licence. (And see 1987 for replacement).

1982. The Deer (Amendment) (Scotland) Act.

1982. The Spring Traps (Approval) Order. (*Protection of Animals Act 1911; Pests Act 1954*).

1982-1987. The Welfare of Livestock (Prohibited Operations) Regulations. Prohibiting certain operations, e.g. hot branding of cattle; de-voicing cockerels; surgical castration of birds. (*Agriculture [Miscellaneous Provisions] Act 1968*).

1983. The Diseases of Fish Act. Re fish farming.

1984. The Slaughter of Poultry (Humane Conditions) Regulations. Slaughterhouse registration. Referring to protection whilst awaiting slaughter. Making compulsory manual back-up to the automatic knife. Exemptions for Muslim and Jewish slaughter. (*Slaughter of Poultry Act 1967; Slaughterhouses Act 1974; Animal Health and Welfare Act 1984*).

1984. Animal Health and Welfare Act. Amends Slaughter of Poultry Act 1967 to apply to all poultry slaughtered for commercial purposes. No specifications re age or ability of slaughtermen.

1984. The Consumer Protection Act. Re animal tests.

1984. The Food Act. Re animal tests.

1984. The Deer (Close Seasons) (Scotland) Order.

1984. The Video Recordings Act. Re cruelty to animals in, in making videos.

1984. The Dangerous Wild Animals Act 1976 Modification Order. Licensing. Zoos, circuses, pet shops and labs exempted.

1985. The Wildlife and Countryside (Amendment) Act. Intention to increase protection for badgers re digging for foxes. Burden of proof shifted to defendants.

1985. The Wildlife (N. Ireland) Order 1985. Making offence of releasing non-indigenous animals into wild.

1985. The Deer (Firearms etc.) (Scotland) Order.

1985. The Food and Environment Protection Act.

1986. The Animals (Scientific Procedures) Act. Animal experiments. Control of procedures which may cause animal pain, suffering, distress or lasting harm. Animals defined as any living vertebrate (other than humans). System of licensing projects, individuals, premises (labs and breeding). Cats, dogs must be purpose-bred (exemptions). Inspectorate. Animal Procedures Committee.

1986. The Dartmoor Commons Act. Husbandry, public access, marks of ownership, unfit animals.

1986. The Control of Pollution (Anglers' Lead Weights) Regulations. (*Control of Pollution Act 1974*).

1986. The Control of Pesticides Regulations.

1986. The Salmon Act.

1987. The Welfare of Calves Regulations. Bannning the veal crate as from 1.1.90, prohibiting crated calf system of veal production. Specifies width of pen must be not less than height of calf at the withers (top of shoulder); the calf must be free to turn round without difficulty; must be fed sufficient iron to maintain full health and vigour, and must have access to sufficient digestible fibre for normal rumen development. (*Agriculture [Miscellaneous Provisions] Act 1968*).

1987. The Welfare of Battery Hens Regulations. Referring to rectifying faulty equipment, to regular inspection of livestock and to space allowances for caged hens. (*Agriculture [Miscellaneous Provisions] Act 1968*).

1987. The Mink (Keeping) Order. (*Destructive Imported Animals Act 1932; Agriculture Act 1947*). Re fur farming.

1987. The Coypus (Prohibition on Keeping) Order. Coypus only allowed for exhibition and scientific (and other) purposes. (*Destructive Imported Animals Act 1932; Agriculture Act 1947; Endangered Species [Import and Export] Act 1976*).

1987. The Consumer Protection Act. Re animal testing.

1988. The Protection Against Cruel Tethering Act. (Amendment to Protection of Animals Act 1911). Making offence of cruel tethering of equines. Also re dog fights, and disqualification from ownership in first cases of cruelty to any species.

1988. The Local Government Act. Stray dogs.

1988. The Spring Traps (Approval) Order. (*Protection of Animals Act 1911; Pests Act 1954*).

1988. The Transit of Animals (Amendment) Order 1988. Covers all animals carried by sea, air, road, rail. (See 1973 above). (*A.H.A. 1981*).

1988. The Welfare of Poultry (Transport) Order. Unspecific on space and length of journey. (*A.H.A. 1981*).

1988. The Veterinary Surgeons (Schedule 3 Amendment) Order. Referring to surgical procedures, mutilations on animals before and after certain ages. (*Veterinary Surgeons Act 1966*).

1989. The Dangerous Dogs Act. Additional powers to courts.

1989. The Tuberculosis (Deer) Order. (*A.H.A. 1981*).

1989. The Firearms (Amendment) Act.

1990. The Slaughter of Animals (Humane Conditions) Regulations. The Slaughter of Animals (Humane Conditions) (Scotland) Regulations 1990. The Slaughter of Poultry (Humane Conditions) (Amendment) Regulations 1990. Slaughterhouse improvements. Restraining of animals heads for more accurate stunning process. Prohibition on use of rotary casting pen (presently used in religious slaughter) as from 5.6.92 in favour of upright restraining pen. Responsibility for enforcing slaughter legislation lies with local authorities at district level (Environ-mental Health Officer and meat inspection team). Scottish legislation different. (*Slaughterhouses Act 1974*).

1990. **The Welfare of Horses at Markets (and Other Places of Sale) Order.**

1990. **Welfare of Animals at Markets Order.** Creating new offence of causing injury or unnecessary suffering to animals at markets. Introducing minimum ages at which calves and foals can be put through markets without their mothers. Banning marketing calves more than twice in any 28-day period. Banning use of electric goads on calves, young pigs, sheep and horses. Prohibiting the tying of poultry and calves. New controls on handling, penning, feeding and watering animals. Welfare officers appointed by market proprietors. Replaces 1964 Order.

1991. **The Movement of Animals (Restrictions) Order.**

1991. **The Welfare of Livestock Regulations.**

1991. **The Environmental Protection Act.**

1991. **The Welfare of Animals at Markets Order.**

1991. **The Welfare of Pigs Regulations.** Phasing out the sow stall and tethering by end of 1998. (Replacing and amending the phase-out period of Sir Richard Body's Pig Husbandry Bill). (*Agriculture [Miscellaneous Provisions] Act 1968*).

The following Bills were at various stages at time of writing.

1991. The Welfare of Animals at Slaughter Bill. (Sir Richard Body MP). Re enabling Minister to implement a number of recommendations made by FAWC Report on the Welfare of Livestock (Red Meat Animals) at the Time of Slaughter.

1991. The Dangerous Dogs Bill. Ban on import and breeding of pit bull terriers and Japanese tosas. Such dogs to be registered, neutered, and muzzled and leashed in public. Insurance. Illegal to sell, advertise, give away, exchange, let stray or abandon. As from 30.11.91. An order to ban also the import of the Fila Braziliera and Dogo Argentina dogs is likely to follow.

1991? Wildlife & Countryside Act 1981 Amendment. Making landowners liable to criminal prosecution for every animal illegally killed. Re killing of species preying on game. (Ron Davies MP).

1991? Badger Bill. Protection for badger sets. (Roy Hughes MP)

1991? Badgers Act 1973 Amendment. (Peter Archer MP).

1991? The Pet Animals (Amendment) Bill. To ban sale by pet shops of animals to children under 16. (David Amess MP).

1991? The Breeding of Dogs Bill. Cracking down on illegal puppy farms, allowing councils to check premises suspected of unlawful use. (Alan Williams MP).

1991? The Hare Coursing Bill. Abolition. (Harry Cohen MP).

Although not law, there are also *The Codes of Recommendations for the Welfare of Livestock* (published by MAFF in separate booklets for cattle, farmed deer, ducks, domestic fowls, goats, pigs, rabbits, sheep, turkeys). The Codes give basic welfare advice to farmers covering housing, feeding etc. Failure to observe the Codes 'shall not of itself render the person liable to proceedings of any kind' but can 'be relied upon by the prosecution as tending to establish the guilt of the accused...'. Also, *Code of Welfare Practice on Abattoir Slaughter of Farm Deer* and the *Guidelines for the Transport of Farmed Deer* (MAFF).

The Council of Europe Convention for the Protection of Animals Kept for Farming Purposes 1976. (Ratified by the UK January 1979). Animals must be housed according to their physiological and ethological needs. Details of EC legislation on livestock are contained in the Official Journal of the European Community, L series.

Single European Market

New legislation is being drafted for the 1992 single market, to allow unrestricted movement of animals between member states. Proposals for *Council Regulations*:

• *for production and placing on market of fresh meat* — improved health standards for slaughterhouse to be implemented by 1993. Current UK 'domestic' or 'export' standards will no longer be allowed. Will mean closure of many slaughterhouses; longer distances for animals.

• *for the disposal and processing of animal waste* — could mean end of knackerman service (calling licensed animal slaughterers to farm to kill and dispose of casualty, sick or injured animals).

• *on protection of animals during transport* — frontier checks only at boundaries of community. May mean animals travelling up to 24 hours without rest, food, water. British law restricts time period to 12 hours. May also mean resumption of trade in live horse export for slaughter.

• *on the protection of animals at the time of slaughter* — individual restraint at time of killing or stunning mandatory.

In the EC at present, the export of livestock for slaughter to Spain and Portugal is forbidden due to their methods of slaughter not being in line with UK standards. This may change with advent of Single European Market 1992.

Also, the European Commission is now proposing that controversial drugs used to boost growth of livestock would be banned if they fail test of social and economic impact. Products such as BST for instance would be assessed to see if they damage livestock, consumer confidence, the environment etc.

Other matters under discussion in Brussels which may or may not lead to Community legislation as Directives or Regulations:

A European Centre for Alternative (non-animal) Testing Methods for Drugs and Cosmetics;

An Advisory Committee on the Protection of Animals used for Experimental and other Scientific Purposes;

Minimum Standards for the keeping of pigs and calves, leading to prohibition of sow stalls and tethers and veal calf crates after 1994;

A Standing Veterinary Committee to oversee transport and slaughter methods;

A Ban on the import of furs from certain species of animals originating in countries where the leghold trap is still in use;

A Draft Directive on Zoos;

A Draft Directive on the Legal Protection of Biotechnological Inventions re the patenting of transgenic animals (life-forms).

Appendix H: *DEATH TOLL*

Table 22. Annual Death Toll in UK (approximate, rounded figures)

Badgers	digging, shooting, clubbing, baiting		10,000
Birds (wild & game)	shooting	grouse	500,000
		pigeon	10,000,000
		partridge	500,000
		pheasant	12,000,000
		snipe	100,000
		wildfowl	1,800,000
		woodcock	150,000
	vivisection		250,000
Cats	destruction		50,000
	vivisection		4,000
Cattle	slaughter		3,500,000
	vivisection		5,000
Dogs	destruction		365,000
	vivisection		10,000
Deer	hunting		350
	shooting		100,000
	slaughter		10,000
Equines	vivisection		1,000
Fish	vivisection		100,000
Foxes	hunting		16,000
	shooting, trapping etc.		300,000
Hares	coursing		1,000
	hunting		7,000
	shooting		300,000
Mink	hunting		800
	slaughter		10,000
Pigs	slaughter		14,200,000
	vivisection		8,600
Poultry	slaughter		700,000,000
Rabbits	shooting		4,000,000
	slaughter		5,000,000
	vivisection		50,000
Sheep	slaughter		20,000,000
	vivisection		15,000
Others	vivisection		3,000,000
Fish	landed by UK vessels		500,000t
	shellfish landed by UK vessels		92,000t
	slaughter (farmed)		70,000t
	shellfish slaughter (farmed)		7,000t

Table excludes goats; camelids; fish killed by angling; other pet species; animals dying in transit; compulsorily slaughtered animals; 'pest' species and others.

GLOSSARY

Baby beef. Meat from fattened, 12-18 month old cattle.

Beastings, Beestings. See **Colostrum**.

Bullock. Castrated bull. Steer.

Bloat (hoven). Distended rumen in ruminants due to grazing on legume-rich pasture and failure of belching mechanism; retention of gasses produced by fermentation in rumen. Gas released by stomach tube or rumen puncture.

Boar. Uncastrated male pig used for breeding.

Bobby veal (slink veal). Flesh from (usually dairy type) calves slaughtered at 1-2 days old. Hence bobby calf.

Bull beef. Beef from uncastrated (entire) male animals.

Buck. Adult male rabbit, fallow deer, roe deer, goat, hare.

Burling. See **Dagging**.

Calving index. Average number of days between calvings. Aim is 365.

Capon. Roasters or roasting bird. Castrated male broiler. Surgical caponization illegal in UK since 1981-2. Now by injection of female hormones.

Chevon. Goat meat.

Cloudburst. False pregnancy.

Colostrum. Mother's first milk, contains extra protein (globulin), antibodies, vitamins and a laxative. Aid to immune system of offspring. Important to newborn in first 3-4 days of life.

Cow beef. Beef from unwanted (infertile or low yielding) cows, for processing.

Creep feeding/grazing. Allowing young animals into pen or field to gain extra feed. Barred entry for older animals.

Crepuscular. Active at dawn and/or dusk.

Crutching. See **Dagging**.

Dagging (crutching, burling). Removal of dirty wool from tail area of sheep, to prevent fly-strike.

Debeaking. Removal of end third of poultry bird beaks by red-hot metal guillotine or snips. Performed as 'remedy' for feather-pecking aggression, cannibalism. Dim lighting is also used to control aggression.

Disgorger. Device used by anglers to remove hook from caught fish.

Doe. Adult female goat, rabbit, fallow and roe deer.

Draft ewe. Sound breeding ewe no longer suitable (e.g. lacking hardiness) for keeping in flock. Draft ewes tend to be sold from hill flocks to lowland farms for further breeding.

Draize eye test. Introduced in 1944. Usually conducted on albino rabbits because their eyes do not produce tears as easily as humans' and cannot wash the test substance away. Substance sprayed or distilled into eye of conscious rabbit, irritancy effects noted for up to 7 days. (And see **VIVISECTION** chapter).

Draize patch test. Hair clipped from an area of skin (guinea pigs or rabbits usually) and sometimes skin abraded too. Test substance taped on and skin observed for signs of damage. As with eye test, painkillers seldom administered.

Drenching. (Oral) dosing of farm animals with liquid medication.

Dystokia. Difficult calving. Arises in approx. 5-10% of dairy cases.

Earth. Fox den.

Efficacy tests. Used when a specific effect is claimed for a product. E.g. anti-plaque properties of dental products tested on mice, rats fed high sugar diet.

Ewe. Adult female sheep.

Ewe (theve, theave) lamb. Female sheep in first year (usually under 6 months), intended for breeding.

Exsanguination. Bleeding out; loss of blood. (See **SLAUGHTER** chapter).

FCR. Food conversion rate, ratio. E.g. 3:1 FCR = 3 units feed needed to produce 1 unit liveweight gain. Alternatively expressed as 3.0.

Farrowing. Sow or gilt giving birth to litter.

Farrowing index. Number of litters produced/year by sow.

Fat (lamb, sheep, cattle etc.). Animals reared for meat, intended and ready for slaughter.

Fawn. Young fallow deer.

Fellmongering. Dealing with leather and wool from dead animals. Preparing for tanning.

Finished. Animals fattened and ready for sale at market; 'fit for slaughter'.

Flushing. Feeding breeding female animals well, e.g. on specially prepared pasture, a month or so before mating, to improve condition and encourage ovaries to produce more eggs. Referred to as (and see) **steaming up** with some species, e.g. fibre goats. 'Flushing' also used as term to describe removal of embryos from one animal for transplanting into another.

Fly strike. Maggots (from blow-fly larvae) in skin and wool of sheep.

Foot rot. Painful, infectious disease in sheep. Causes lameness. Common on wet land. Similar condition found in pigs.

Freemartins. Rare. When heifer and bull calves are born as twins, heifer calf is known as a freemartin. Sterile in 9 cases out of 10. (So will not be kept for breeding).

Gaff. Device used usually by game anglers for landing large fish. Stout hook, mounted on a staff, impaled through jaw or body.

Gag. Device used by anglers to keep pike's mouth open whilst retrieving hook(s).

Gilt. Young female pig up to weaning of first litter.

Gimmer. Young female sheep, between first and second shearing. (See **Sheep**).

Goatling. Female goat between 1 and 2 years old.

Grilse. See FISH FARMING .

Halal. Muslim (ritual) religious slaughter, no prior stunning. Refers also to the meat from same.

Harbourer. Person who studies movements of deer, locating suitable animal for hunt.

Havier. Castrated deer (N. Ireland).

Heifer. Female cow, over one year old. Will be called a cow after her second calf.

Heifer calf. Female bovine under 1 year old. Cow calf.

Hind. Adult female red deer.

Hinny. Offspring of she-ass by stallion.

Hog. Castrated male pig reared for slaughter.

Hogg, Hogget. Male (but sometimes female) sheep between weaning and first or second shearing. (See **Sheep**).

Hoven. See **Bloat**.

In-bye. Fenced area on sheep farm incl. farmhouse, holding ewe flock in winter, and for dipping, shearing etc.

In vitro. Literally, in glass. Refers to experiments performed in test tubes etc; non-animal tests.

Joint-ill. See **Navel-ill.**

Keet. Young guinea fowl.

Kelt. Salmon after spawning. For other salmon terms see FISH FARMING.

Knacker. Slaughterer.

Kid. Young goat up to 1 year old. MAFF Codes consider goats under 6 months to be kids.

Kindling. Term for rabbit parturition.

Kosher. Food deemed acceptable for Jewish consumption. (See SLAUGHTER).

Lamb. Name for young sheep until one year old. In some areas, until 6 months. Mainly, until weaning. MAFF Codes consider sheep under 6 months to be lambs.

Maiden heifer. As yet unmated female cow.

Mare. Female horse, 5 years old and over.

Middlings. Wheatfeed for livestock.

Milt. Roe of male fish.

MOET. Multiple ovulation and embryo transfer. Artificial breeding technique.

Moult. Towards end of first year of laying, hen's ovulation ceases, old feathers replaced by new. Being unproductive at this stage, hen usually slaughtered.

Mule. Cross-bred sheep, from Border Leicester ram and a hill ewe. Also offspring of male ass and mare or she-ass and stallion: hinny. General term for hybrid.

Mulesing. Australian mutilations (named after inventor, JHW Mules) of sheep. Breech Mulesing: removal of wool, skin and flesh around anal area to combat fly-strike. Other Mulesing operations deal similarly with pizzle (penis) and jowl areas.

Mutton. Meat of older sheep, now sold mostly for manufacturing and processing.

Navel-ill, Joint-ill. Infection through animal's unhealed navel. Prevented by hygiene and by dressing navel and cord with antiseptic at birth.

Nurse Cow. A cow used to suckle calves not her own. In the course of a lactation she may suckle 3-10 calves.

Outlier. Carted deer hunted but not caught on the day. (N. Ireland). Also, livestock kept outside in winter.

Ox. Most often, a castrated male bovine. Steer.

Parturition. Act of giving birth.

PMSG. Pregnant mares serum gonadotrophin. Used for promotion of out of season breeding (induction of oestrus) in various farm animal species.

Porge. Remove blood and lymph vessels and nerves from meat carcase.

Point of Lay. Stage at which pullet about to start laying eggs.

Pollard. Animal from which horns have been removed.

Polled. Naturally hornless individual animal of horned species.

Pot ale. By-product of whisky distillation, often added to animal feed.

Poult. Young turkey, under 8 weeks.

Poussin. Spring chicken. Slaughtered at approx. 7 weeks.

Priest. Club used by anglers to administer *coup de grâce* to game fish. And used generally in fish slaughter.

Pullet. Female fowl, in first laying year.

Purse seine. Fishing net of encircling type drawn together underneath shoal of fish. Usually big catches of fish for fishmeal.

Raddling, Ruddling. Marking ram on breast with coloured iron oxide powder to leave mark on rump of ewes tupped or covered (mated). Marking colour sometimes carried by harness fitted to ram.

Ram (Tup, Tip). Uncastrated adult male sheep. Often pure bred to pedigree. Kept for breeding.

Ram lamb. Male sheep in first year, intended for breeding.

Rig. Male sheep with one or both testicles undescended, or improperly castrated.

Rut. Especially of male deer. Sexual excitement; urge to mate. Seasonal.

Scab. Skin disease. Also known as mange.

Scours. Forms of diarrhoea, due to faulty feeding, poor management or infection. Symptom of diseases.

Scrapie. Neurological disease in sheep. Fatal. (And see **Appendix B: BSE**).

Seining, Seine-netting. Fishing method whereby fish herded into trawl-type net fixed between 2 long warps which close as the vessel moves forward.

Set, Sett. Badger's burrow.

Shearling. Sheep shorn once. Usually in second year. Ewes which have not yet had first lambs.

Shechita. Jewish (ritual) religious slaughter, no prior stunning. By shochet.

Sheep. Only some of the vast range of names used for sheep are included here. For a more complete glossary the reader is advised to consult an agricultural or veterinary dictionary.

Shochet. Trained Jewish slaughterman, licensed by Chief Rabbi.

Smolt. Young salmon. See **Kelt**.

Smothers. Poultry dead on arrival at slaughterhouse due to shock, stress, heat, cold, suffocation.

Snood. Pendulous skin over turkey's beak.

Sow. Female pig after having or weaning first litter.

Stag. Adult male red deer. Adult male turkey over 26 weeks.

Stallion. Uncastrated (entire) male horse, 5 years or older. Kept for breeding.

Steaming Up. Feeding cow or heifer well (addition of concentrates to normal ration) during last 6-8 weeks of pregnancy in order to encourage future milk production. Also with in-lamb ewes prior to lambing. And other species.

Steer. Castrated male bovine over 1 year old. Bullock.

Sticking. Throat-cutting and bleeding-out of livestock at slaughterhouse.

Stirk. Male and female cattle under 2 years old (Scotland). Females only in England; males called steers.

Stock ewe. Ewe over 5. Kept on for breeding as especially valuable.

Stores. Animals kept on low level of growth for later fattening.

Strike. See **Fly-strike**.

Stripping. Extracting milk remaining in cow's udder. Pressing, squeezing out the ripe roe or milt from a fish. By hand.

Suckler cow. Cow which suckles own calf and then reared for beef.

Teg. See **Wether** and **Hogg**. Also ewe teg; female sheep from weaning to shearing.

Terrier men. With terrier dogs, used by fox hunts to bolt or dig fox from earth or similar refuge.

Toxicity testing (incl. **LD50** and **LC50**): Involves force-feeding animals (usually rats and mice) with substance under test to ascertain damaging effects. LD50 = Lethal dose for 50% of the animals in test. LC50 (Lethal concentration which kills 50% of animals in test) involves forcing animals to inhale sprays, dusts, vapours.

Trash fish. Commercial fish catch not used for human consumption but for farmed fish and other livestock feed — direct or in meal.

Trefah. Food deemed unacceptable for Jewish consumption. (See **SLAUGHTER** chapter).

Trolling. Fishing method whereby vessel tows a number of lines on or at various depths below surface using lures or bait to attract fish to kooks.

Tufter. Experienced staghound.

Tup, Tip. See Ram.

Tup ram. Uncastrated male lamb, up to weaning. Ram lamb.

Tupping. Sheep mating.

Weaner. A weaned piglet (3-5 weeks nowadays) under 10 weeks old, i.e. prior to fattening.

Wedder. See Wether.

Wether, Wedder, Teg. Castrated adult male sheep intended for slaughter. 12+ months old. Castrated male goat.

Weatings. See Middlings.

Yearling. Animal in second year of life.

Yeld. Dry or barren animal not producing milk. In shooting terms, yeld hinds refers to deer which have no calves at foot; immature hinds, or those failing to breed the previous year.

Yolk. Fatty secretion from skin (sebaceous glands) of sheep; wool-oil.

REFERENCES

Country Sports: Animals
1   Bird population figures from L. A. Batten *et al. Red Data Birds in Britain.* Nature Conservancy Council/RSPB (T & AD Poyser 1990).

Country Sports: Falconry
1   *BBC Wildlife,* April 1991.

Country Sports: Hunting
1   *Observer,* 1.7.90.
2   *The Guardian,* 5.11.90/14.12.90.
3   Huw Griffiths. *On the Hunting of Badgers.*(University of Wales 1991).

Country Sports: Shooting
1   *Fowl Play,* Channel 4 TV, 3.2.91.
2   *The Guardian,* 7.3.91.
3   *Death by Design* (RSPB 1991).
4   Ian Presett CBE, in Shooting Birds. League Against Cruel Sports leaflet, 1991.
5   *Fragile Earth: The Egg Detectives,* Channel 4 TV, 8.4.91.
6   *The Guardian,* 4.9.90.
7   *Observer,* 14.10.90.
8   *The Guardian,* 6.10.90.
9   Hunt Saboteurs Association. 1990. Figures correlate with those from *Sport Shooting in the UK* by John Harradine in *Working Group on Game Statistics.* (Eds.) F. Leeuwenberg & I. Hepburn (International Union of Game Biologists. Netherlands. 1983). Table shown amended by figures from *Guns Review,* December 1990. Shotgun and firearms certificate figures are Home Office latest (1989).
10 Scottish figures from *The Economic Impact of Sporting Shooting in Scotland.* (British Association for Shooting and Conservation 1990).

Farmed Animals: Breeding & Feeding
1   *Animal Deaths in Agricultural Buildings* (RSPCA 1988).
2   From Andrew Tyler. *The Independent on Sunday.* 7.90.
3   *Profit from Progress.* Genus Marketing. (Milk Marketing Board 1990).
4   Countryside & Agriculture. Friends of the Earth leaflet. 7.90.

5   *Farm Journal* (*Press & Journal*, Aberdeen), 1.9.90.

Farmed Animals: Land Use Table
1   Figures extracted and calculated from *Agriculture in the UK* 1989 and 1990 (HMSO 1990 and 1991). Reproduced with permission of Controller of HMSO.
2   1990 figures are provisional.
3   Figures do not include land used for buildings, roads etc. on livestock farms.

Farmed Animals: Cattle
1   *Agriculture in the UK* 1989 and 1990, and *Agricultural Census June 1990 Final Results*. All 1990 figures provisional. Reproduced with permission of Controller of HMSO. And see **Introduction**.
2   *Farm Journal* (*Press & Journal*), 1.9.90, reporting forecast made by Prof. John Nix, Dept. of Agricultural Economics, Wye College, in a report on the future structure of dairy farming, commissioned by BOCM Silcock.
3   Graham Boatfield. *Farm Livestock* (Farming Press 1986).
4   *Sunday Times*, 21.4.91. *The Guardian*, 22.4.91.

Farmed Animals: Goats
1   Scottish Cashmere Producers Association figure for 1990 de-haired weight. Gross weight was 531.5kg.

Farmed Animals: Pigs
Population, slaughter and output figures reproduced with permission of Controller of HMSO.
1   *Farmers Weekly*, 1.6.90.
2   From James Erlichman in *The Guardian*, 29.6.90.

Farmed Animals: Poultry
Population, slaughter and output figures reproduced with permission of Controller of HMSO.
1   Figures for minor holdings are included for England & Wales but not for Scotland and N. Ireland.
2   Pimental & Pimental. *Food, Energy & Society* (Edward Arnold 1979).

Farmed Animals: Sheep
Population, slaughter and output figures reproduced with permission of Controller of HMSO.

1 *Observer*, 24.3.91.
2 *Observer*, 1.7.90.

Farmed Animals: Slaughter

Population, slaughter and output figures reproduced with permission of Controller of HMSO.

1 *The Guardian*, 22.8.90.
2 *Scottish Farmer*, 15.9.90.
3 Humane Slaughter Association, *Annual Report* 1989-90.
4 *Agscene* 102, Spring 1991.

Sea Fisheries

All landing figures reproduced with permission of Controller of HMSO.

1 *Observer*, 2.6.91.
2 David Armstrong. DAFS scientist. Quoted in *Fishing News*, 3.5.91.
3 *The Guardian*, 28.8.90.
4 *Observer Scotland*, 22.5.90.
5 Article 13 of Council Regulation (EEC) No. 3926/90. 20.12.90.
6 Freshwater Fisheries Laboratory *Annual Review* 1988-89 (DAFS).
7 *The Guardian*, 13.5.91.
8 *Fishing News*, 10.5.91.

Fish Farming

1 MAFF estimate, December 1990.
2 *Veterinary Record*, 11.5.91.
3 MAFF estimate, November 1990.

Animals Performing

1 *Say yes to the highest standards of animal welfare.* Association of Circus Proprietors brochure 1991.
2 *Animals in Circuses.* RSPCA.

Pets

1 From *Profile.* Pet Food Manufacturers Association 1990 and 1991.
2 Baker Audits of GB 1987.
3 Stephen Young in *The Guardian*, 3.8.90.
4 *Sunday Times*, 1.7.90.
5 *Indiscriminate Dog Breeding and Dealing* (RSPCA, KC, BVA, BSAVA, 1989).

6 Animal Control in the UK. St Andrew Animal Fund leaflet.

7 *Observer*, 8.7.90.

8 From *The Costs of Stray Dogs and Proposals for a National Dog Registration Scheme: A Report for the RSPCA* London School of Economics and Political Science 1989.

9 *Analysis of Major Areas of Concern for Animal Welfare*. RSPCA 1989.

Pets: Humane Destructions Table

1 All figures from the PCAs' Annual Reports 1989 and 1990 and correspondence. According to 8 above, 90,000 stray dogs/year are destroyed by or on behalf of (mostly by the RSPCA) the Police. These are separate from the tally of dogs abandoned by their owners at vets or shelters and subsequently destroyed. Total destructions of other species unknown.

Vivisection

1 *The Guardian*, 5.2.91.

2 Robert Sharpe. *The Cruel Deception* (Thorsons 1988).

3 *Code of Practice for the Housing and Care of Animals Used in Scientific Procedures* (HMSO 1989).

4 Robert Sharpe. 'Designed to Kill', in *Outrage* 68, 1990.

5 *The Guardian*, 8.4.91.

6 *Sunday Times*, 14.10.90.

Vivisection Tables

All statistics reproduced with permission of Controller of HMSO.

1 Table from Dr Hadwen Trust for Humane Research; selected figures compiled from *Statistics of Scientific Procedures on Living Animals Great Britain* 1989 and 1990 (HMSO 1990 and 1991).

2 Selected figures from above *Statistics*.

3 Selected figures from *Statistics of Scientific Procedures on Living Animals Northern Ireland* 1989 and 1990. (HMSO 1990 and 1991).

Zoos

1 European Survey of Zoos. Zoo Check 1987.

2 Malcolm Whitehead, Director of Education, Twycross Zoo, in letter to *BBC Wildlife*, October 1990.

3 Captive Polar Bears in the UK and Ireland, in Zoo Check Report 1985.

REFERENCES

Appendix A: Illegal Cruelty
1   All statistics from the Annual Reports of the SPCAs.

Appendix B: BSE
1   Ray Bradley, MAFF central veterinary laboratory, reported by Robin McKie in *The Observer*, 22.4.90.
2   *The Guardian*, 31.5.90.
3   *Sunday Times*, 13.5.90.
4   *Sunday Times*, 27.5.90.
5   John Wilesmith, head of epidemiology unit, MAFF central veterinary laboratory, reported in *The Observer*, 2.9.90.
6   *British Meat*, Spring/Summer 1990. *The Guardian*, 22.11.90, 12.12.90, 1.2.91, 28.3.91, 26.4.91, 30.7.91.

Appendix C: Export & Import
1   *The Guardian EG*, 18.9.90. Agscene 101, Nov/Dec 1990.
2   *Farmers Weekly*, 1.6.90.
3   *Animal Health* (HMSO 1990).
4   *Business Monitor: Overseas Trade Statistics of the UK*. Central Statistical Office. (HMSO 1990). Reproduced with permission of Controller of HMSO/CSO.
5   *Sunday Times*, 12.5.91.
6   James Erlichman in *The Guardian*, 20.5.91.
7   Natural World. *Sunday Times*, 30.6.91
8   Mortality Rates in Imported Birds. MAFF News Release, 20.2.91.
9   *Press & Journal*, 12.2.91.
10 RSPCA Annual Report 1990.
11 Customs & Excise 18.3.91.
12 From UK Trade Statistics 1989:Imports of CITES-listed animals and animal products, prepared by Wildlife Trade Monitoring Unit, Cambridge.

Appendix E: UK Exotics
1   All information from 'Escaped exotic mammals in Britain', Simon J Baker, in *Mammal Review* 1990, Vol 20, Nos 2/3, 75-96. (Blackwell Scientific Publications)
2   *Observer*, 16.12.90.

BIBLIOGRAPHY

The publications listed below are those which have been consulted for general information. Some may also be found incorporated into the text where relevant, or in REFERENCES when specific data have been quoted. The listing should serve also as recommended reading for those seeking further information on any of the foregoing topics.

ALDERMAN, D.J. & WICKENS, J.F. *Crayfish Culture*. Laboratory Leaflet 62. (MAFF Fisheries Research, Lowestoft 1990).

ANON. 'The Cosmetics Industry'. *Outrage* 68. 1990.

BAKER, S. 'Escaped exotic mammals in Britain'. *Mammal Review* 1990. Vol 20, Nos 2/3, 75-96.

BATTEN, L.A., BIBBY, C.J., CLEMENT, P., ELLIOTT, G.D., PORTER, R.F. (Eds.)*Red Data Birds in Britain*. Nature Conservancy Council/RSPB. (T & AD Poyser 1990).

BLAXTER, K. & CUNNINGHAM, J.M.M. *et al. Farming the Red Deer*. (DAFS/HMSO 1988).

BOATFIELD, G. *Farm Livestock*. (Farming Press 1986).

CHARLTON, J. & JACKSON, T. *Field Sports*. (Stanley Paul & Co. 1984).

CLOUGH, C. *The Animal Welfare Handbook*. (In preparation).

COOPER, M.E. *An Introduction to Animal Law*. (Academic Press 1987).

CRAWFORD, J. *Kill or Cure*. (ARC Print 1988).

DALAL-CLAYTON, D.B. (Ed.) *Black's Agricultural Dictionary*. (A & C Black 1985).

DAVIDSON, J. 'Hunting Partners'. *Country Living*, January 1991.

DRUCE, C. *Chicken & Egg: Who pays the Price?* (Green Print 1989).

EGAN, G.
  'Fish-Farming'. *Outrage* 66. 1990.
  'The Pharmaceutical Industry'. *Outrage* 72. 1991.

EYTON, A. *The Kind Food Guide*. (Penguin 1991).

GILES, T. 'Through Troubled Waters'. *The Guardian EG*. 20.11.90.

GILL, R. Dept. of Zoology, Cambridge. 1990. *Monitoring the Status of European and N American Cervids*. Report for Global Environment Monitoring System/UN.

GOLD, M.
  Assault & Battery. (Pluto Press 1983).
  Living Without Cruelty. (Green Print 1988).

GOULD, J. (Ed). *Deer Farming: A Handbook for the 1990s*. (British Deer Farmers Association 1989).

GWYTHER, M. & MILLINSHIP, W. 'Unnatural Acts'. *Observer* magazine. 16.12.90.

HALLEY, R.J. & SOFFE, R.J. (Eds.). *The Agricultural Notebook*. (Butterworth 1988).

HARRADINE, J. 'Sport Shooting in the UK: Some Facts & Figures'. In*Working Group on Game Statistics*. Proceedings of the Second Meeting, 6-7 October 1982. Leeuwenberg, F & Hepburn,I. (Eds.). (IUGB. Netherlands. 1983).

HOWLETT, L. *The Cruelty-Free Shopper*. (Bloomsbury 1989).

JOHNSON, W. *The Rose-Tinted Menagerie*. (Heretic Books 1990).

KOHN, M. 'Me and My Bird'. *The Guardian*. 1.12.90.

LAIRD , L. & NEEDHAM, T. (Eds.). *Salmon and Trout Farming*. (Ellis Horwood 1988).

LANGLEY, G.
(Ed.). *Animal Experimentation: The Consensus Changes*. (Macmillan 1989).
'Drug Tests on Animals'. *Outrage* 61. 1989.
'The Question of Pain and Suffering'. *Outrage* 62. 1989.
'Warfare and Space Research'. *Outrage* 63. 1989

LEOSCHKE, W.L. *Feeding and Nutrition of Mink*. (Hoffman-La Roche & Co).

MACKENZIE, D. *Goat Husbandry*. (Faber 1980).

MARCHANT, J.H. *et al*. *Population Trends in British Breeding Birds*. (British Trust for Ornothology 1990).

MCKENNA, C. 'The Fur Trade'. *Outrage* 65. 1990.

MCKENNA, V; TRAVERS, W; WRAY, J. (Eds.). *Beyond the Bars: the Zoo Dilemma*. (Thorsons 1987).

MITCHELL, B. *et al*. *Ecology of the Red Deer*. (Inst. of Terrestrial Ecology 1977).

NILSSON, G. *et al*. *Facts About Furs*. (Animal Welfare Institute USA. 1980).

PAGE, J. 'London Zoo'. *Outrage* 70. 1990.

PARKER, C. & THORNLEY, J. *Fair Game*. (Pelham Books).

PILKINGTON, E.
'Hunting'. *The Guardian EG*. 15.1.91.
'Zoos'. *The Guardian EG*. 23.4.91.

PIMENTEL, D. & M. *Food, Energy and Society*. (Edward Arnold 1979).

PORTSMOUTH, J. *Commercial Rabbit Meat Production*. (Saiga Publishing 1979).

PRICHARD, M. (Ed.). *Encyclopaedia of Fishing in Britain and Ireland*. (Collins 1982).

RUESCH, H.
Slaughter of the Innocent. (Futura 1979).
Naked Empress. (CIVIS 1982).

RUSSEL, A. 'Goats for Milk Production.' *In Practice*. September 1990.

RYDER, R.D.

  Animal Revolution: Changing Attitudes Towards Speciesism. (Blackwell 1990).

  Victims of Science. (NAVS 1983).

SAINSBURY, J.C. *Commercial Fishing Methods*. (Blackwell Scientific 1986).

SANDFORD, J.C. *The Domestic Rabbit*. (Granada 1979).

SHARMAN, P.R.J. *Poultry*. (Association of Agriculture 1978).

SHARPE, R.

  'The Case of Corwin'. *Outrage 70*. 1990.

  'Catalogue of Cruelty'. *Outrage 70*. 1990.

  The Cruel Deception. (Thorsons 1988).

  'A Degree of Compassion'. *Outrage 69*. 1990.

  'Designed to Kill'. *Outrage 68*. 1990.

  'The Human Factor'. *Outrage 72*. 1991.

  'Over the Limit'. *Outrage 63*. 1989.

SHEPHERD, C.J. & BROMAGE, N.R. (Eds.). *Intensive Fish Farming*. (BSP Professional Books/Blackwell Scientific Publications Ltd 1988).

SPEDDING, C. (Ed.). *Fream's Agriculture*. (Murray 1983).

SOPER, M.H.R. *Studies with Sheep*. (Association of Agriculture 1989).

STOKER, H. *The Modern Sea Angler*. (Robert Hale Ltd 1987).

SWEENEY, N. *Animals and Cruelty and Law*. (Alibi 1990).

TUCK, A. 'Fishing for Insults'. *Time Out* 10-17 October 1990.

TYLER, A. 'Hi-Tec Animals'. *Independent on Sunday* 7.90.

VINES, G. 'Safari Parks, after the honeymoon'. *New Scientist* 2.12.82.

WARWICK, C. *Reptiles: Misunderstood, Mistreated & Mass-marketed*. (Trust for the Protection of Reptiles 1990).

WHEELER, H.L.H. *Pigs*. (Association of Agriculture 1978).

WYELD, H.R. & H. *Ducks & Geese*. (HMSO 1980).

Those documents listed unitalicized below are leaflets, papers etc. rather than retail publications.

ADAS Advisory leaflets (various dates).

Agriculture in the UK 1989 and 1990. (MAFF/HMSO. January 1990 and 1991). No annual statistics published by MAFF for rabbits, camelids, fur animals, deer.

MAFF evidence to the House of Commons Select Committee on Agriculture, Overview of Aquaculture, 1.11.89.

Guidance on the Operation of the Animals (Scientific Procedures) Act 1986, HMSO (1990; HC182).

Agricultural Statistics for the UK 1990. (HMSO 1991).

Report of the Animal Procedures Committee 1989 and 1990. (HMSO '90 and '91).

Analysis of Major Areas of Concern for Animal Welfare. (RSPCA 1989).

Bloodsports in Britain. The St Andrew Animal Fund.

1989 Survey of Crayfish production in England. (MAFF).

Animals in Circuses. RSPCA.

Information Relating to the Use of Council Land by Circuses with Performing
    Animals. Animal Aid.

The Captive Animals Protection Society *Annual Report* 1987-8, 1988-89, 1989-90.

Animal Deaths in Agricultural Buildings. (RSPCA 1988).

Code of Practice for Shooting Deer. Red Deer Commission. (HMSO 1986).

Countryside Sports: Their Economic Significance. Report for the Standing Conference
    on Countryside Sports. (Cobham Resource Consultants 1983).

Damage by Deer. Red Deer Commission. (HMSO 1986).

Functions and Policies. Red Deer Commission. (HMSO 1986).

Red Deer Management. Red Deer Commission. (HMSO).

Roe Deer: Management & Stalking. (Game Conservancy).

Intensive Egg, Chicken & Turkey Production. (Chicken's Lib. 1990).

Farm Animal Welfare Council Reports (HMSO).

  The Slaughter of Poultry (1982).

  Welfare of livestock (red meat animals) at the time of slaughter (1984).

  Welfare of livestock when slaughtered by religious methods (1985).

  Welfare of Farmed Deer (1985).

  Egg Production Systems; An Assessment.(1986).

  Welfare of Livestock at Markets (1986).

  Assessment of Pig Production Systems (1988).

  Statement on Mink and Fox Farming (1989).

  Handling and Transport of Poultry (1990).

  Animals slaughtered by Jewish and Muslim methods. (1990).

Management & Welfare of Farm Animals. Universities Federation for Animal Wefare.
    (Bailliere Tindall 1988).

Output & Utilization of Farm Produce in the UK. (HMSO).

1989 Survey of Fin Fish Farms in England. (MAFF).

Report of the SOAFD Annual Survey of Fish Farms for 1990.

Freshwater Fisheries Laboratory *Annual Review.* 1988-9 (DAFS).

Marine Laboratory Aberdeen *Annual Review* 1988-9 (DAFS).

The Game Conservancy Review of 1989. (Game Conservancy 1990).

Animal Health 1989. The Report of the Chief Veterinary Officer (HMSO 1990).

Bailey's Hunting Directory 1990/1991. (J.A. Allen & Co).

The Laboratory Animals Buyer's Guide. (Royal Society of Medicine Services Ltd).

Statistics of Scientific Procedures on Living Animals, Great Britain 1989 and 1990. (HMSO. July 1990 and 1991).

Statistics of Scientific Procedures on Living Animals, Northern Ireland 1989 and 1990 (HMSO 1990 and 1991).

Halsbury's Laws of England, Halsbury's Statutes, Halsbury's Statutory Instruments. (Butterworth).

Marine Fish-farming in Scotland. (Scottish Wildlife & Countryside Link. 1988).

Mink Factories. (Lynx & Compassion in World Farming. 1988).

Report of the Animal Procedures Committee 1989 and 1990 (HMSO 1990 and 1991).

Profile. (The Pet Foods Manufacturers' Association 1990 and 1991)

Review. (World Wide Fund for Nature 1990).

Salmon Farming. DAFS. January 1991.

A Code of Practice for the Housing and Care of Animals used in Scientific Procedures, (HMSO 1989: HC107).

Sea Fish Industry Authority *Annual Report* 1990.

Sea Fisheries Statistical Tables 1989(HMSO 1991).

Scottish Sea Fisheries Statistical Tables 1989 (HMSO 1991).

Shellfish Farming. Quarterly literature listing. (SOAFD Sept '90 and March '91).

Shellfish Farming in Scotland during 1989. (DAFS Marine Lab).

Report of the Panel of Enquiry into Shooting & Angling (RSPCA 1980).

The Economic Impact of Sporting Shooting in Scotland. Fraser of Allander Institute, Strathclyde University. (British Association for Shooting & Conservation/ Scottish Development Agency 1990).

Slaughter of Livestock for Meat? (Humane Slaughter Association 1990).

UK Trade Statistics 1989. Wildlife Trade Monitoring Unit, Cambridge 1991.

Codes of Recommendations for the Welfare of Livestock. (MAFF 1990).